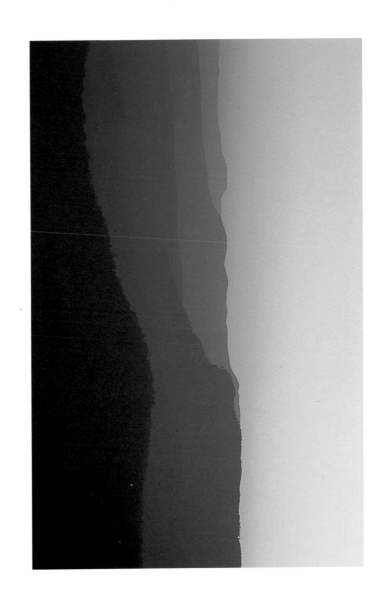

AUSTRALIA

A Continent Revealed

First published in 1996 by
New Holland Publishers (Australia) Pty Ltd
Sydney • London • Cape Town

Produced and published in Australia by
New Holland Publishers (Australia) Pty Ltd
14 Aquatic Drive, Frenchs Forest,
NSW 2086 Australia

24 Nutford Place, London W1H 6DQ
United Kingdom

80 McKenzie Street, Cape Town 8001
South Africa

Copyright © in text: Neil Hermes
Copyright © in captions: Anne Matthews
Copyright © in maps: New Holland Publishers
(Australia) Pty Ltd
Copyright © in photographs: individual photographers
and their agents as listed on p. 224
Copyright © in published edition 1996: New Holland
Publishers (Australia) Pty Ltd

Reprinted: 1997, 1998

All rights reserved. No part of this publication may be reproduced, stored in a retrieval system or transmitted, in any form or by any means, electronic, mechanical, photocopying, recording or otherwise, without the written permission of the publishers and copyright holders.

ISBN 1 86436 206 5

Senior Designer **Trinity Fry**
Editor **Thea Coetzee**
Publishing Manager **Mariëlle Renssen**
Picture Researchers **Anne Matthews
and Vicki Hastrich**
Illustrator **Annette Busse**

Reproduction: cmyk prepress, Cape Town
Printed and bound by: Tien Wah Press (Pte) Ltd,
Singapore

Front cover Moonrise over the Bungle Bungle massif in the Purnululu National Park in Western Australia.
Half title page A pair of kangaroos in the grasslands at Cossack in Western Australia.
Previous pages, left An aerial showing the picturesque Whitehaven beach, which forms part of the Whitsunday Islands in Queensland; right Twilight over the Blue Mountains National Park in New South Wales.
Right The ancient red rocks contrast with the waters of Gantheaume Bay near Broome in Western Australia.
Following pages A solitary figure on the vast dry saltpan of Lake Eyre South in South Australia.

CONTENTS

The AUSTRALIAN CONTINENT

Australia consists of two landmasses, the mainland and Tasmania, which are separated by the Bass Strait. It is 24 times the size of the British Isles, covering 7 682 300km² (2 965 368 sq miles). Lying in the southern hemisphere it stretches 3983km (2475 miles) east–west and 3138km (1950 miles) north–south with a coastline totalling 36 735km (22 827 miles). The surrounding oceans are the Timor and Arafura seas in the north, the Pacific in the east, the Southern in the south and the Indian in the west. Papua New Guinea is Australia's nearest neighbour and lies 200km (124 miles) north from Cape York, across the Torres Strait.

Often referred to as the flattest continent, Australia comprises three major physiographic regions: the Eastern Uplands, the Interior Lowlands and the Western Plateau. These regions are dissected by the Tropic of Capricorn. This vast area and its varied conditions mean that the climate differs enormously across the continent. With just over one-third of the country lying in the northern tropical zone, heavy rainfalls occur during the 'Wet' (summer) season. The southern zones are temperate or Mediterranean and receive most of their rainfall during the winter months. The Centre, however, is a vast arid zone which is not affected by off-shore moisture and cold fronts, and receives minimal rainfall. Here temperatures soar during the day and drop sharply at night.

Australia is divided into six states (Queensland, New South Wales, Victoria, Tasmania, South Australia and Western Australia) and two territories (the Northern Territory and the Australian Capital Territory). The population of Australia is estimated to be 18 million which translates to a density of only two people per square kilometre. However, 85 per cent of the population lives in the fertile urban areas of the continent, predominantly on the eastern seaboard.

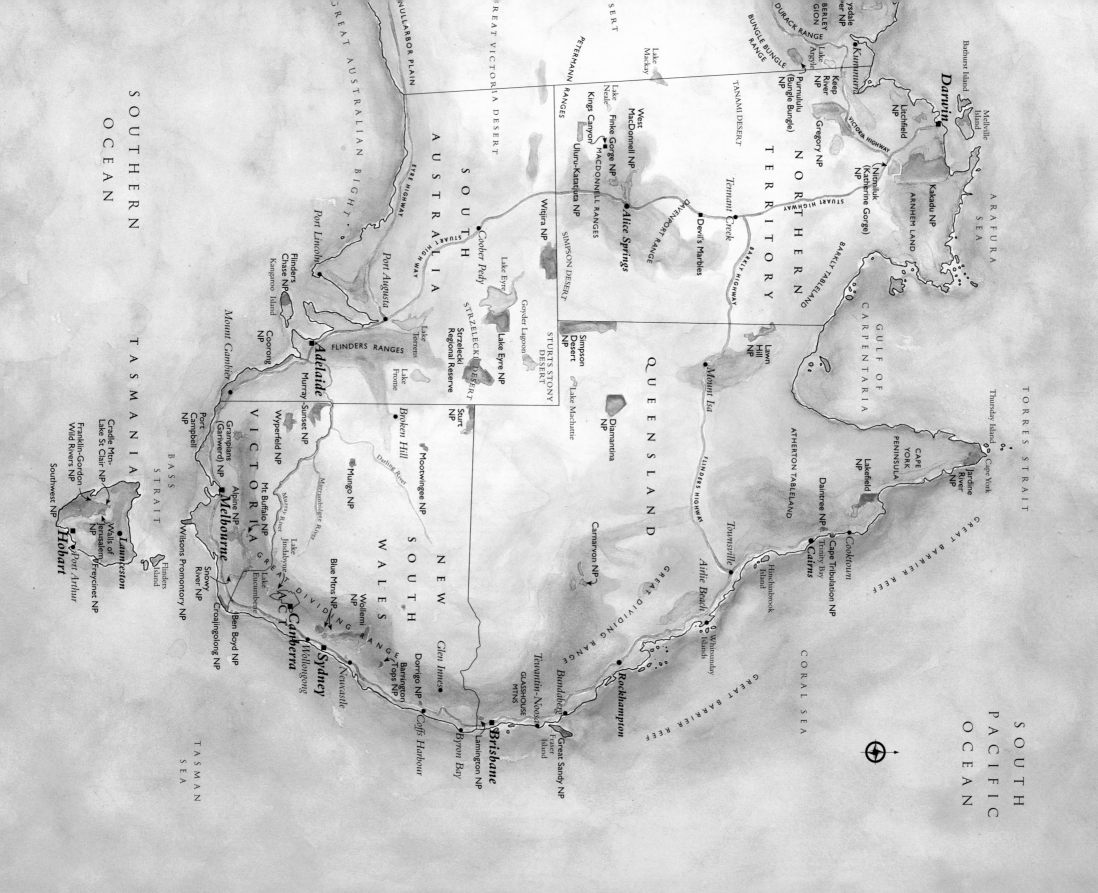

A CONTINENT EVOLVES

The human spirit is drawn to the unusual and distinctive. In an increasingly homogenous modern world we seek variety: we praise people and places, countries and continents for their uniqueness, their differences; not for their similarities. Australia is a land of such refreshing individuality. It is a magnificent continent boasting rich contrasting landscapes, exciting and exotic flora and fauna, and a truly multicultural population.

Literally 'southern land', Australia is a continent set apart from the rest of the world – it drifted away from the supercontinent, Gondwana, over 45 million years ago. This long isolation, like being cut adrift on an ark, combined with the turbulent changes of the past 200 years, makes Australia both ancient and timeless, new and exciting. You have only to contrast modern Australia, home to one of the world's youngest, most vibrant and multicultural people, with the indigenous population, who remain one of the planet's oldest and most traditional cultures, to see the evidence of this.

Unlike our modern quest for difference, Australia's early European settlers searched the landscape in vain for the familiar. It is evident from their drawings and paintings that these were artists trained in another world. They struggled with what they saw in the new continent – they rounded the sharp and tortured shapes of the trees; depicted the natural blues and greys of the foliage in more conventional greens; and the distant blue horizons were misrepresented in green or brown. These artists futilely attempted to recreate, at least on canvas, the old world in the southern hemisphere. The true and unique character of the new land was suppressed, and the yearning for home was not restricted to the artists alone.

A desire for the familiar was also demonstrated by the names the new settlers bestowed on the native flora and fauna. Birds were called robins, warblers and magpies, despite a complete lack of biological relationship with their northern namesakes. Indigenous trees erroneously became known as oaks, ashes and cedars. And when these strange trees, birds and animals, even with their new and comforting names, did not behave in appropriate ways, familiar ones were introduced. Animals such as foxes, rabbits, hares, pheasants, nightingales and goldfinches, to name a few, were imported to bring previously everyday sights and sounds to a strange and seemingly hostile landscape. The most in-appropriate plants, such as oaks, roses and tulips, were cultivated in waterless, seasonless parts of the continent. Many of these introductions survived with assiduous help, but others could not overcome the resilience of the new land, its challenging climate and native flora and fauna. Unfortunately, some newcomers, like blackberries, starlings and rabbits, have thrived on their own, rapidly outliving their role as reminders of home and creating environmental havoc in their adoptive land.

Such relatively modern impacts on the Australian continent are, however, merely the final paragraphs in the latest chapter of a long and very complex geological and environmental story.

Left Eucalypts are popularly called 'gum trees' and there are over 500 species in Australia. On mountain ridges snowgums are often twisted by the effects of strong wind, especially during periods of low temperature. They form bizarre shapes on the landscape, like this strikingly beautiful one in the southern Victorian Alps.

IN THE BEGINNING – AN ANCIENT LANDSCAPE

Australia is an extraordinary ark: a unique, part-ancient and part-modern blend of landscapes, plants and animals. On the land's western side, facing the Indian Ocean, lies the mountainous desert region known as the Pilbara. Also in the west, but looking out on the Southern Ocean, are the rugged granite coasts of the Albany area. One of the largest and oldest pieces of the earth's surface joins these two areas, a great fragmented shield of country over 1000km (621 miles) across. These hard, twisted rock formations were folded and compressed by herculean forces early in the planet's geological history. Today in the Pilbara you can walk around the low, craggy hills and pick up a piece of rock that is 3000 million years old.

With the exception of those ancient Pilbara landscapes, much of the land has undergone a process of constant change. Over the millennia large tracts of the continent's original land surface have been altered many times. There have been cycles of ocean flooding, inland seas appearing, eroding and subsiding, volcanic activity, and a slow persistent twisting of the surface. Even the shape of the continent as we know it today was not created until comparatively recently, as Australia's overall modern outline was only formed about 45 million years ago when the continent finally broke away from Antarctica and then headed north in the long Gondwana breaking-up process.

The physical features of Australia today have been moulded by periods of time so extensive that they defy human conception. When the earth formed, its surface was molten rock and had not yet solidified into a crust. The first signs of life appeared 3.6 billion years ago, but were restricted to single-celled organisms for most of the next 3 billion years. Although some of them clustered together to form structures (the fossilised forms are called stromatolites), true multicellular organisms did not appear until 600 million years ago. These appear to be jellyfish-like with no hard skeletons. Fossils do not become abundant until an event known as the Cambrian Explosion (a palaeontological term referring to an 'explosion' of life), which occurred around 550 million years ago. Dinosaurs ruled the earth from 220 million to 65 million years ago, and the first humanoids appeared in Africa only within the last million years.

Above The upland Pilbara region of mid-north Western Australia contains some of the world's oldest rocks rich in gold, iron ore and other valuable minerals. However, this barren red rock and the earth support little vegetation other than hardy plants such as spinifex, a spiny grass that covers most of the outback. Trees like this snappy gum (a small, drought-resistant eucalypt) somehow manage to survive in the arid conditions.

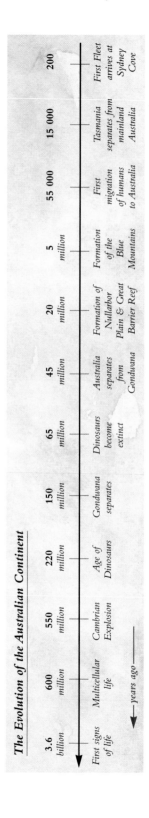

The Evolution of the Australian Continent

3.6 billion	600 million	550 million	220 million	150 million	65 million	45 million	20 million	5 million	55 000	15 000	200
First signs of life	Multicellular life	Cambrian Explosion	Age of Dinosaurs	Gondwana separates	Dinosaurs become extinct	Australia separates from Gondwana	Formation of Nullarbor Plain & Great Barrier Reef	Formation of the Blue Mountains	First migration of humans to Australia	Tasmania separates from mainland Australia	First Fleet arrives at Sydney Cove

← years ago ——

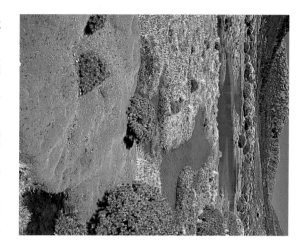

Above Although cut off from the mainland 15 000 years ago, Tasmania's highland region is part of the Great Dividing Range. The uplands contain rugged peaks and hills, lakes and superb vegetation. The Walls of Jerusalem National Park supports wet grass-lands and a wide range of subalpine flora, including these spongy cushion plants that thrive in the moist conditions.

Below Australia's sandstones have been eroded over time to form spectacular cliffs and rock formations. The dramatic 300m-high (984ft) Arnhem Land escarpment (the eastern border of Kakadu National Park) is one such famous feature, and the park itself contains isolated sandstone outcrops, such as this at Nourlangie Rock, which is also an important Aboriginal art site, featuring figures painted in 'X-ray' style.

While some parts of the Australian landscape were moulded and formed very early in the history of the earth, most of the major landforms that we recognise today were formed 'relatively' recently. The Great Barrier Reef and the Nullarbor Plain formed around 20 million years ago. The gorges of the Blue Mountains were being carved around 5 million years ago and Bass Strait became flooded, isolating Tasmania from mainland Australia, only 15 000 years ago.

Against the history of the earth, the history of people in Australia is almost insignificant. The earliest findings of Aboriginal settlement in Australia occur around 40 000 years ago, and the First Fleet was sent from England to set up a penal settlement in the new colony called New South Wales just over two centuries ago.

A great deal of imagination is required to appreciate the time taken to shape the continent overall, but a quantum leap is necessary to attempt to understand the earth's forces that created the landforms as we know them today. The pressures that were necessary to force up the original Flinders Ranges in South Australia to the height of the modern-day Himalayas defy the imagination, as do the forces that eroded these hills down to their low, craggy modern appearance.

The Formation of Sandstone

Sandstone cliffs are some of the continent's most dramatic and well-known natural features. This rock is created when mountains are worn down and rivers dump vast amounts of the resultant gritty deposits in nearby lakes and seas. Over vast periods of time, the loose marine sands compact and solidify; the seas drain away and a new coarse rock – sandstone – is formed. Around 1600 million years ago, massive mountain ranges were being eroded in areas of Gondwana that were later to form part of the Australian continent, and two of the country's most famous sandstone formations – the cliffs of Kakadu in the Northern Territory and the domes of Western Australia's Bungle Bungles – were laid down at this time.

Aeons later, about 600 million years ago, a similar process of sedimentation was underway in a bay of a great inland sea. In this case a dense grey sandstone monolith was formed, which was to become the country's most recognisable rock: Uluru. This massive form was eventually twisted through an angle of 90° and the sandstone now stands upright, surrounded by a sea of red sand. The original grey rock has become stained by the sand's iron minerals and, like a beacon, Uluru shines red in the central desert twilight as it has done for tens of millions of years.

By comparison, the sandstone cliffs of Sydney Harbour and the Blue Mountains, west of the city, are young – only 220 million years old! Sydney's sandstone overlays a bed of economically important older sediments. Beneath coastal New South Wales, the Hunter Valley and a vast area of central Queensland lie deep (in places the seam is over 200m, or 656ft, thick) rich coal deposits which have helped Australia to become the world's largest exporter of black coal.

The Creation of Volcanic Landscapes

Volcanic activity has been an important component of the continent's geological past. The most recent volcanic eruptions, although small, occurred less than 5000 years ago around the coastal-border lands of South Australia and Victoria. The rich agricultural soils and volcanic landscapes, such as the 'spectacular Blue Lake at Mount Gambier, are the result of these episodes. The greatest volcanic eras, however, occurred much longer ago and the most obvious features of these periods are the vast deposits of richly coloured and beautifully shaped granites.

The famous granite coasts of Albany in Western Australia, Kangaroo Island in South Australia, the very aptly named Devil's Marbles in the Northern Territory, and Queensland's Glasshouse Mountains are all the result of different periods of great volcanic activity. It is not only the windswept cliffs and the bizarre shapes of eroded boulders, however, that owe their great beauty to coloured granites. Several famous man-made structures, such as the pylons which support the Sydney Harbour Bridge and the great entrance wings of the nation's Parliament House in Canberra, are beautifully clad in granites which come from the volcanic regions of Moruya and Eugowra in New South Wales.

Rugged Mountains and Valleys

Although some Australian mountains were created by volcanic activity, the peaks and ranges were more often formed by continental pressures of inconceivable force. Many of these geologically 'new' mountains were once two or three times taller than their modern forms, and it is a measure of the great age of the Australian continent that few high peaks remain. In Australia, the craggy peaks that are so typical of other continents have been worn down dramatically by the erosive forces of wind and rain over many millenia.

As mountains were pushed up by continental forces, deep valleys were also formed. Over long periods of time, the mountains became eroded, creating vast sedimentary deposits which then filled the valleys. These sediments were then cemented by various mineral growths to form new rocks. Further continental forces uplifted these rocks so they were again exposed to erosion and the whole cycle began again. This continual process of mountain and valley formation resulted in the creation of some of the country's most rugged and dramatic mountain environments. The tortured and twisted desert formations of the beautiful MacDonnell Ranges in central Australia, and the Flinders Ranges to their south, are testament to these complex and archaic geological cycles.

Left Granite rocks and cliffs, the result of ancient volcanic activity, appear at numerous places along the continent's southern shores. The granite coastline around Albany in Western Australia, for example, is famous for its weathered cliffs, but here these high, rugged promontories are interspersed with coves, bays, white sandy beaches and crystal-clear blue waters. The boulders and outcrops at Little Bay, west of Albany, have been rounded and smoothed by the relentless pounding of the Southern Ocean waves.

Below A rather bizarre rock formation is found far inland in the Northern Territory. Aboriginal legend refers to these often precariously balanced boulders as the 'Eggs of the Rainbow Serpent'. The Devil's Marbles are actually remnants of a once large, but now almost completely eroded, granite outcrop. The rocks often glow with a dramatic fiery colour at sunset.

THE EVOLUTION OF AUSTRALIA'S UNIQUE FLORA & FAUNA

In keeping with the Australian continent's ancient and different landscape, the abundant wildlife is unsurpassed in its variety and ingenious adaptation to the unique environment. Several of Australia's plants and animals have, through their long isolation from the rest of the world, developed their own very special forms.

The land that became the new continent of Australia was once part of Gondwana, which also encompassed Antarctica, South America, Africa and India. Gondwana began to break up 150 million years ago and Australia finally split from Antarctica some 45 million years back. The plants and animals that now inhabit

Australia are a blend of the descendants of those shared with the other Gondwana continents, those that have evolved here, and others that have since crossed the oceans. Some Australian animals, such as koalas and kangaroos, once existed on the other Gondwana continents, but more advanced mammals evolved

on those continents, and the new species superseded the marsupials. The new mammals, such as bears and cats, were kept out of Australia by its ocean barriers and Australia's marsupials endured. This fascinating survival story has been repeated for many other uniquely Australian plants and animals.

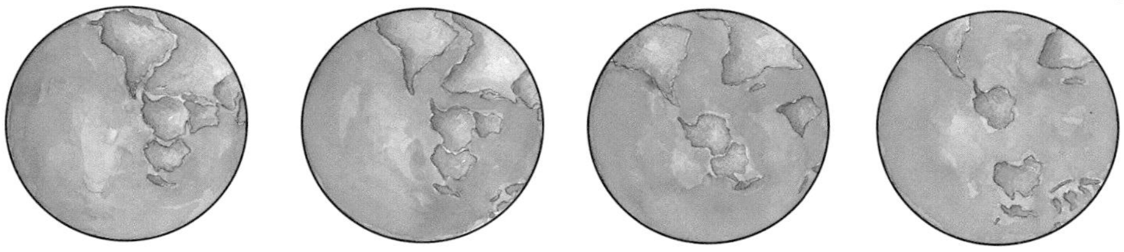

Primitive Plant and Animal Forms

South-west of Western Australia's Pilbara region, near where some of the world's oldest rocks can be found, there are modern survivors of the planet's most ancient living things. Growing in a warm and secluded inlet of Shark Bay is a colony of bizarre primitive life forms. Stromatolites are generally known as the fossilised remains of algae colonies, yet most of those found here are still alive and active and resemble a cluster of dark, rounded rocks. Fossils of these unique creatures, dated at over 3500 million years old, have been found in other parts of Australia and around the world, but in the bay's secluded and oxygen-depleted waters these extraordinary life forms continue to survive. When the ancestors of these algae first evolved, the earth's atmosphere was almost devoid of oxygen and many biologists believe that stromatolites and their relatives, over many millions of years, released enormous amounts of oxygen into the earth's atmosphere. This activity changed the primitive, carbon-dioxide-rich atmosphere of the earth to the oxygen-rich atmosphere we have today. In a sense, all advanced life may well owe its oxygen-rich existence to the forebears of these early life forms.

An arid corner of the Australian continent was the site of one of the world's great evolutionary discoveries. Just as the animals of the Galápagos Islands were instrumental in the formation of Charles Darwin's concepts of evolution, a young Australian geologist was inspired in the rugged desert mountains of South Australia. In 1947, Reg Sprigg discovered strange fossils in the low Edicara Hills of the Flinders Ranges which proved to be evidence of the earliest multicellular animals ever known. These fossils of ocean-living animals included sponges, sea jellies and sea worms that were over 600 million years old. Until Sprigg's discovery, it had been generally believed that no fossils of this age or form would ever be found — after all, these soft-bodied species were 99 per cent water, had no hard skeletons or shells and would be unlikely to form recognisable fossils. The ancient sandstone ranges also form the rim of one of South Australia's most impressive landforms — Wilpena Pound's 10km-wide (6 miles) natural amphitheatre.

Australia separates from Gondwana

Above Millions of years ago Australia formed part of the supercontinent of Gondwana which also comprised Antarctica, South America, Africa, Madagascar, New Guinea, New Zealand and the Indian subcontinent. While there is some dispute about the timetable for the break-up of the supercontinent, it is commonly believed that the rupture was caused by the mechanisms of continental drift.

Above Dating back many millions of years, the stromatolites at Hamelin Pool in Western Australia's Shark Bay are unique survivors of the world's most primitive life forms. Although they appear to be rocks, these stromatolites are actually living things — they are slow-growing spongy plants that have been formed by tiny single-celled algae.

Invertebrate marine organisms suddenly became prolific in the event known as the Cambrian Explosion around 550 million years ago. Many different types of organisms that secrete shells of calcium carbonate, including corals, some types of sponges and some bivalves, have periodically formed huge reef structures. With the passage of time, these reefs have become the various limestone deposits we see today. In modern times, the percolation of fresh water through the limestone has led to the formation of famous caves at Chillagoe in north Queensland, and Jenolan and Bungonia in New South Wales.

Age of the Dinosaurs

Australia had its own 'Jurassic Park'. The geological period after which the movie was named dates back to around 150 million years ago, but many of Australia's giant reptiles belonged to more recent geological periods. Muttaburrasaurus, the skeleton of which was found near the town of Muttaburra in central Queensland, for example, was an 8m-long (26ft) herbivorous dinosaur. Parts of another dinosaur's neck found in the same region come from a massive animal that was over 20m (66ft) long. One of Australia's most interesting prehistoric fossils are the

footprints of 130 small dinosaurs at Winton in Queensland. These chaotically arranged prints reveal a moment of fear for the tiny herbivorous creatures as they were chased across a mudflat by a larger carnivorous dinosaur. It seems that they all escaped, but the incident was firmly recorded in what is now solid rock.

Evidence of Australia's earliest mammal came in the late 1980s with the discovery of the opalised jawbone of a 110 million-year-old relative of the platypus. Found at the New South Wales mining centre of Lightning Ridge, this remarkable discovery set the scene for the evolution of Australia's familiar but unique monotremes (egg-laying mammals of which only the platypus and echidna exist in Australia) and marsupials (mammals with an external pouch within which newly born offspring develop, such as koalas, kangaroos and their many relatives).

A now unfamiliar, but typically Australian, creature evolved around 2 million years ago and survived until as recently as 20 000 years ago. Australia was home to a variety of giant pouched mammals known as the marsupial megafaunas. Some of these were the size of water buffalo, while others had elephant-like trunks. The marsupial leopard hunted herds of grass-eating species such as the 3m-high (10ft) giant kangaroos, while flamingos shared this landscape with crocodiles and half-a-dozen species of koalas. The giant marsupials disappeared well after the arrival of the Aboriginal people on the continent, some 40 000 years ago, and whether their disappearance was due entirely or only in part to human activity is still in dispute. Changes in climate, for example, may have been another factor that could have driven these giant and bizarre life forms to extinction but, hopefully, time and science will unravel more of this mystery.

Top Australia is home to around 600 reptile species, one of the most spectacular of which is the frilled lizard. Found mainly in the north and north-east, it raises its impressive 'frill' when handled or attacked.

Above left The rarely seen platypus is one of Australia's strangest and most primitive mammals. Although warm-blooded and covered in hair, it is a monotreme.

Above centre The fearsome saltwater (estuarine) crocodile is widespread in the seas and rivers of northern Australia. Growing to 6m (20ft) in length, these aggressive 'crocs' will attack anything from snakes and birds to wallabies, and even humans.

Above right The chunky, lumbering wombat is an appealing creature. These nocturnal herbivores are found in Tasmania and in the mainland's south-east, and like other marsupials they have well-developed pouches to carry their young.

Creatures of Australia's Ark

The world's most dangerous creature and the largest living reptile, the estuarine or saltwater crocodile, inhabits the continent's tropical northern waterways. Growing to more than 7m (23ft) in length, this distant relative of the dinosaurs is protected and has in recent years been brought back from the verge of extinction.

Australia is fortunate in being at least a part-time home to six of the world's seven species of sea turtles. Large numbers of these wanderers, the most well-known of which are the loggerhead turtles of Mon Repos in central Queensland, breed on Australia's tropical beaches in summer.

Despite the variety and richness of its other animals, Australia's strange, beautiful mammals are probably the continent's most important 'ambassadors'. From the unlikely egg-laying platypus and echidna to the marsupial koalas, possums and kangaroos, the continent's mammals are symbols of the country. Australia boasts almost 50 different kinds of kangaroo and wallaby, ranging from tiny rat kangaroos to the great red, which can be over 2.5m (8ft) high and can weigh as much as 85kg (187 lb). Some kangaroos are rock dwellers and several species live in trees. All kangaroos are plant eaters, but certain other marsupials are carnivorous.

The probably now extinct Tasmanian tiger (the last confirmed sighting was in the 1930s) was the largest of the modern meat-eating marsupials. Still common, however, is the fierce-looking Tasmanian devil, which has replaced the Tasmanian tiger as the largest carnivorous marsupial. One of the smallest meat-eating marsupials is the yellow-footed antechinus, which weighs about 50g (1.75oz) and is found in bushland around the cities of the east coast. These tiny, energetic creatures have a rapid metabolism and are constantly on the lookout for food – insects, small birds or lizards. In spring, the mating urge leads the antechinus to copulate when it is 12 months old. The required effort is too much for the males, who die within days of mating. The females produce up to a dozen young a month later and live free of male competition for food. Mothers and youngsters separate the following winter for the cycle to begin again.

Half of the world's 20 most lethal snakes live on the Australian continent, and of the 100 or more species of native snakes, about one-quarter are considered to be dangerous to humans. The world's second-largest lizard, the perentie, grows to over 2.5m (8ft) in length and is at home in much of the continent's arid inland. These deserts are the richest place on earth for many lizard species, which range from the giants (goannas) to the fastest (skinks) to the most spectacular (frilled lizards) and the most bizarre (thorny devils). Another strange Australian creature is a diminutive frog which raises its young in its stomach. This peculiar baby-rearing behaviour makes the gastric brooding frog unique in the entire animal kingdom.

With the exception of South America, Australia is home to the world's largest populations of distinctive birds. The Australian bush is vibrant with the sights and

Top The 'cute' koala is everyone's favourite marsupial, but these cuddly looking creatures have sharp teeth and claws and can be quite aggressive. Related to wombats, these endangered tree-dwellers are found only in eastern Australia and live on eucalyptus leaves.

Above left The Macropodidae family of kangaroos and wallabies forms one of the continent's most abundant fauna types. The red kangaroo, occurring in Australia's drier regions, is the largest of these.

Above centre There are several varieties of rock wallaby; these kangaroo relatives are well adapted to life in rugged terrain. Their broad feet and mobile tail help them to balance as they leap from rock to rock.

Above right The yellow-footed antechinus is widespread in eastern Australia. These nocturnal predators sleep in underground nests by day and hunt for insects, spiders and small vertebrates such as mice at night.

Above The eucalyptus, or gum tree, is the most prominent and distinctive character of the Australian landscape. It constitutes about 95 per cent of the forest and woodland trees. The majority of the species grow in the coastal regions but some varieties have adapted well to the semiarid sand plains of central Australia.

Below Derived from African baobabs, Australia's boab trees are found only in the far north and are a particularly common sight in Western Australia's Kimberley region. Although rarely growing above 12m (39ft) in height, the bulbous trunk is designed to store water and nutrients during times of drought and can be as much as 20m (66ft) in diameter.

sounds of over 700 bird species – from colourful, raucous cockatoos and parrots to diminutive fairy wrens. The continent is well known for its nightly 'penguin parade' (from the sea to their burrows) on the picturesque Victorian coastline, and for the daily visits of rainbow lorikeets to feeding stations in the eastern seaboard forests. Also famous are the calls of some species, such as the friendly chortle of the kookaburra and the persistent 'ringing' of bellbirds.

Millions of years of isolation have endowed Australia with some bird-world scientific wonders: included in this category are the flightless emu and cassowary, the sound-mimicking lyrebird, the broad-billed nocturnal frogmouths, and the bowerbirds. The males of the latter species build the most elaborate structures, known as bowers, not for nesting but in fact to attract females.

It is easy to see how the birds, mammals and other animals of the 'great south land' can be likened to creatures on an ark. Their unique behaviour and appearance are a result of the continent's peculiar habitats and its long isolation from the rest of the world. Much has been discovered, but it is likely that many more bizarre, yet highly successful, adaptations are still to be revealed.

A Unique Plant Heritage

Australia boasts an assemblage of plants unlike those of any other continent: about 80 per cent of the 20 000 native plant species are found nowhere else on earth. From towering forest gum trees to the bright red banksias of the coastal scrubs, the continent's variety of flora is of great beauty, antiquity and value. The origins of certain Australian plants can be traced back to the continent's ancient links with the other southern landmasses. The towering southern beech, found in the cool mountains of Tasmania and eastern Victoria, has a pollen fossil history extending as far back as 60 million years. Kauri pines, which include the Norfolk Island pine and the bunya and hoop pines of Queensland, have close relatives in South America, New Zealand and parts of the Pacific.

Australia's most conspicuous plants are the eucalypts, or gum trees as they are commonly known. These trees, along with wattles, dominate most landscapes, with the exception of the rainforests and the coastal margins. Eucalypts range from forest giants such as the mountain ash to arid land mallees, which are little more than desert shrubs. The majestic mountain ash, found in Victoria and Tasmania and reaching a height of up to 100m (328ft), is one of the world's tallest species of tree, exceeded in height only by the towering Californian redwoods. The mallees, on the other hand, compensate for their diminutive stature with spectacularly coloured red, yellow and orange flowers.

As a mere reminder of much larger alpine areas of past geological times, Australia offers a small but beautiful range of alpine flora. Plants such as the large anemone buttercup and early flowering purple alpine hovea are scattered on the glaciated granites and loose sediments at the foot of 2228m-high (7310ft) Mount Kosciusko in New South Wales, the nation's tallest peak. The heathlands of the southern coasts contain quite a profuse diversity of endemic plants such as banksias, hakeas and grevilleas, which are hardened to regular and intense bushfires and very well adapted to the poor soils. The tropical north is home to the curiously shaped boab tree. This squat tree is named after its extraordinarily bloated and sometimes hollow trunk; although it is usually relatively short, it can sometimes reach a height of up to 12m (39ft). This rotund life form, one of Australia's few native deciduous trees, stores water in its fibrous trunk and flour can be made from the seed pods and their seeds. One particularly spacious boab tree near Derby in Western Australia was actually used as a jail during the last century!

ONE SMALL STEP: AUSTRALIA'S FIRST HUMAN INHABITANTS

The full colour and character of a continent is only partly revealed by its landscapes, plants and animals. Its human inhabitants complete the scene, and the people of Australia present a long and extraordinarily diverse history.

There are several theories as to the origins and approximate arrival date of Australia's first inhabitants. What is clear, however, is that Aborigines are descended from people who lived in south-east or eastern Asia, and that their migration route to the continent was by island-hopping through what is now Indonesia. These first Australians were undoubtedly very capable mariners. Australia has never been connected to Asia by a land bridge and it is thought likely that humans first reached the continent by simple ocean-going craft such as canoes or rafts.

The earliest migrations must have taken place at least 50 000 years ago: this timing is derived from clear evidence of human occupation of parts of southern Australia from around 40 000 years back, and allows for gradual colonisation of the continent from the north. Archaeological records confirm that most of the continent was occupied by at least 30 000 years ago, and even the harshest corners by 10 000 years after that time. Also very relevant is the fact that around 50 000–55 000 years ago sea levels were much lower and the gaps between the Indonesian islands were narrower than today, making marine crossings far less treacherous.

What is not clear is how many migrations occurred and when they started. Was there one single colonisation as late as 50 000 years ago, or has the continent seen a number of waves of settlement by different groups of humans? Archaeological evidence is ambiguous. Some scientists believe that the skeletons of early Australians reveal

two or more types: some are a heavy, archaic variety and quite different to those of modern Aborigines. These scientists suggest that there may have been some very early arrivals, who were later supplanted by a new wave of migrants.

Lake George, in southern New South Wales and close to the nation's capital, Canberra, provides tantalising evidence of possible human habitation of the continent in far earlier times. The lake has no natural outlet and its water level therefore rises and falls in cycles, depending on the amounts of rainfall and evaporation. The bed of the lake has remained undisturbed for millions of years and sediment up to 30m (98ft) deep has slowly accumulated. Leaves, flowers and pollen from the bushland of the surrounding hills were laid down with these sediments: the flowers and leaves rapidly decomposed on the floor of the lake, but the tiny, distinctive pollen grains have survived. By identifying, in each layer of sediment, the species of plants to which the pollen grains belong, it is possible to observe changes that occurred over long periods of time in the composition of the forests surrounding the lake. Similarly, charcoal from different layers of the lake provides an indication as to the frequency of fires at different historical times.

From these studies it has been suggested that humans, with their firesticks, changed the landscape around the site of modern-day Canberra over 100 000 years ago. This evidence is, however, only circumstantial and the oldest known human occupation sites in the region date back a mere 25 000 years. Meanwhile, the quest to discover the earliest dates for Australia's human occupation continues, as do attempts to unravel the intriguing story of migrations to the continent.

Above Although no-one is certain, it is generally agreed that Aboriginal people first arrived on the continent from south-east or eastern Asia at least 50 000 years ago. With the exception of visits to the northern coasts by South-East Asian fishermen, and the occasional landing of European explorers and seafarers, Australia's Aborigines lived an undisturbed life of nomadic hunting and fishing until the arrival of the British soldiers, convicts and settlers in 1788.

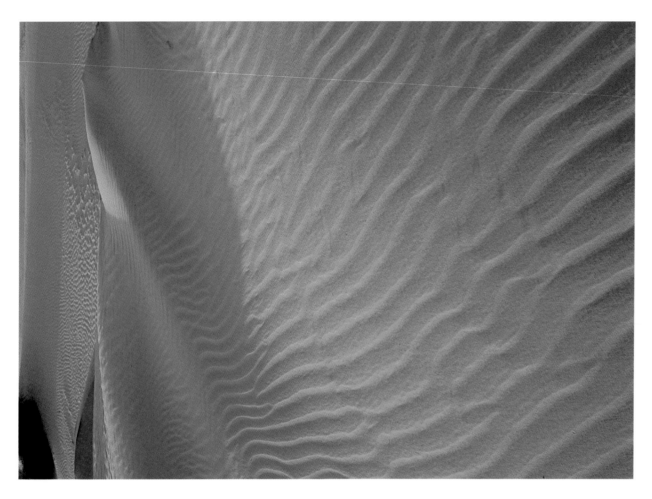

Above It seems almost incredible that Mungo National Park, in the arid outback of New South Wales, was once the site of vast freshwater lakes and abundant animal and Aboriginal life. The park, part of the Willandra Lakes World Heritage region, now contains large stretches of sand dunes and dry salt lakes, dotted with only the most hardy vegetation. This area has yielded some extraordinary archaeological riches – evidence of ancient Aboriginal life and rituals that dates back 40 000 years.

Evolution of an Aboriginal Culture

Discovered in southern New South Wales in 1975, 'Mungo Man', who died about 30 000 years ago, is the oldest and most complete human skeleton found on the continent. His remains were discovered among evidence of a landscape rich in food, including freshwater mussels and fish, which is surprising as Lake Mungo is now a salt lake, devoid of water and located 400km (249 miles) from the sea. We know, however, that when Mungo Man lived the lake was one of a string of large, deep, inland freshwater lakes. Large Aboriginal communities lived on the lake shores at that time – in winter they harvested food from the surrounding deserts, and during summer they depended heavily on the lakes for sustenance. These people cremated the decorated bodies of their dead, possessed 'technologies' to collect fish and small mammals, and used stone tools and fireplaces. The complex ritualistic and symbolic life of the Aboriginal people living on the banks of Lake Mungo about 30 000 years ago offers suggestions of, and links to, the cultural depth of modern-day traditional Aboriginal life.

Over 200 different Aboriginal languages were spoken at the time of European settlement in 1788, but this number increases to more than 800 if all the variations and dialects are included in the tally. Traditionally, these languages were never written – the 'law' and the 'knowledge' was passed from generation to generation through spoken stories. Aboriginal Australians were firmly bound together by their cultural roots, the geography and natural history of the land, trade and customary beliefs, and their 'creation stories', an extremely important aspect of their culture and one which crossed the boundaries of all the different language groups in the same way as prized pearl shells, ochres and hatchet stones.

Creation stories are fundamental to the belief systems and customary law of all Aboriginal societies, and although the detail varies from place to place, these stories exhibit many common patterns. A very widespread concept that forms the basis of many of them is that of the creator beings who moved across the land creating all landforms and living things. There is quite a strong connection between the creator beings and people who are dead, living and of the future, with custodial obligations being formed between the dead and the living. The creator beings and the stories revolving around them are understood at many levels, and knowledge of these levels becomes part of the rite of passage during the life span of each individual on earth; these rites of passage may be quite different for men and women. The shared physical, intellectual and spiritual

Below Ancient Aboriginal art, in the form of rock paintings and engravings, is found in many parts of Australia. The styles and content vary considerably, but the subject matter frequently includes fish, snakes, goannas, kangaroos, people, and strange figures from the spirit world. These vividly coloured murals are located in the remote Keep River National Park, on the border of Western Australia and the Northern Territory.

elements of the creation stories between the legends of neighbouring peoples provide connections to a wider society, and all knowledge, law and understanding are drawn from a complete familiarity with this belief system. This spirituality is given a variety of names, and each language has its own precise vocabulary to identify it. In English it is often referred to as 'Dreamtime' or the 'Dreaming', but this is an expression that many Aboriginal people would rather not use. The appropriate regional Aboriginal name is often preferred – in central Australia, for example, the name *tjukurpa* is the correct description. Similarly, different regional names are used to refer to indigenous Australians: in central Australia the Aboriginal people may refer to themselves as *anangu* or *yapa*, whereas in Sydney and the surrounding area the expression *koori* is generally preferred.

As Governor Arthur Phillip raised the English flag at Sydney Cove on 26 January 1788 and took possession of half the continent of Australia as the new colony of New South Wales, some of the local Aboriginal population looked on. At that time Phillip estimated that 1500 Aboriginal people inhabited the coastal bays around Sydney. It has long been believed that the population of the continent in 1788 was approximately 300 000 people, but more recent research suggests that there were as many as 750 000 Aboriginal inhabitants.

The indigene followed different traditions and customs in various parts of the continent. In the Sydney area, and in much of coastal southern Australia, Aborigines lived in groups of up to 100 people with a population density of about one person for every 2km² (0.77 sq miles). Groups on the north and south sides of Sydney Harbour spoke different languages and some had little, if any, contact with each other.

The land was rich in foods all year round: each group required a relatively small area in which to exist and there was no need to travel far to collect the main foods of fish, shellfish, small mammals, berries and fruits. Both men and women fished, the men with spears and the women with nets and lines. However, as was common in most Aboriginal societies, it was the women who collected the bulk of the food.

Regular use was made of shelters along the water's edge and large hills of discarded shells, called middens, accumulated: there is still ample evidence of these along the coast. Tools included spears, boomerangs and fishing lines. Canoes up to 5m (16ft) long were made of pieces of bark from stringy-bark trees strapped together.

Around the harbour stone engravings of animals and anthropomorphic figures were abundant. These, probably representing ancestral beings, were deeply grooved into the sandstone rock surfaces.

Above The common brush-tailed possum was once a highly favoured food source for Aboriginal people, but this marsupial is now so widespread that it is sometimes considered a pest. These possums occur in and around most Australian cities where they nest in tree holes of suburban gardens and even the roof spaces of houses.

Above The bogong moth is a member of the Noctuidae moth family which is dull-coloured and whose larvae include the highly destructive army worms and cut-worms. Once, however, the metamorphosed larvae were a much sought-after delicacy of the highland Aborigines of southern New South Wales. The name 'bogong' is an aboriginal word for 'large moth'.

Aborigines of the Highlands

The highland Aborigines, or 'moth-hunters', of the southern New South Wales mountains occupied much larger territories than their coastal kin due to the seasonal and relatively less abundant food sources. One person in the highlands may have required up to 50km² (19 sq miles) of living space. Several large tribal groups, including the Walgalu and Ngarigo, occupied much of what is now the New South Wales Monaro Plains and Snowy Mountains. A clan might have consisted of 20 men, women and children, and as these people had to move regularly to sustain themselves, they travelled lightly and had few possessions. Light overnight huts were made of the bark of red stringy-bark trees, but more substantial structures were erected when food was abundant in a particular area.

Women were equipped with a digging stick, wooden food-collecting bowls and possum-skin coats to combat the often cool mountain climate. Men carried clubs, boomerangs, spears and perhaps a stone axe, and usually wore a skin coat. Some of the spears in this region were unlike those from other areas: the long wooden shaft was edged at the tip with up to a dozen sharp quarz flakes that stopped the spear from retracting when flesh, either animal or human, was impaled on it.

The principal year-round food of the highland Aboriginal tribes was kangaroo, brush-tailed possum and birds such as ducks and black swans, while emu flesh was regarded as particularly palatable. In summer, river fish such as the Murray cod or Macquarie perch were speared, or drugged by the narcotic effects of tea-tree or hickory bush leaves. The permanent rivers yielded other delicacies in the form of yabbies (freshwater crayfish), platypus and shellfish. Women collected the wide-spread yam daisies, which had rootstocks that could be eaten either raw or roasted. Acacia seeds were also collected and, unlike the practice in other regions, these were eaten raw rather than crushed into flour.

The annual food highlight for highland Aborigines, and the reason they were known as 'moth-hunters', was the summer migration to the moth grounds of millions of post-hibernation bogong moths. The moths would flock to the granite crevices of the high country ranges in the Tinderry, Brindabella and Bogong mountains of Victoria and southern New South Wales. These fat adult moths were smoked from their hiding places, roasted in hot ash beds and, after dextrous winnowing to remove the ash and grit, eaten in huge numbers. The moths provided a windfall for mountain Aborigines, some of whom walked hundreds of kilometres to join the feast. On such occasions, the normally socially isolated bands of people would come together in groups of many hundreds.

The moth-hunting season was also a very special time of trading and ceremony. Large stone arrangements, or bora rings, on exposed granite slopes were important initiation and spiritual places. Ochre paintings are still found in rock shelters at some of these sites, but their style and extent are not on the same scale as in northern Australia. Ceremonial battles and intermarrying were also integral parts of the great moth harvest.

Aborigines of the Tropical North

In northern Australia, for example in the region that is the home of the Gagudju people – now Kakadu National Park – Aboriginal life was quite different. Non-Aboriginals regard the tropical north as having two seasons – the 'Wet' from November to April and the 'Dry' from May to October – but at least six main seasons were identified in one of the Aboriginal languages, with each linked to the abundance of food in different places. *Yegge*, the cool but humid time from May to June, was followed by the cool dry *Wurrgeng* and the hot dry *Gurrung* seasons.

Right Located in the far north of the Northern Territory, Kakadu National Park lies well within the tropics. Although the seasons here are divided into the 'Wet' and the 'Dry', the climate is relatively hot, humid and damp for most of the year, giving rise to extremely lush forms of vegetation. Kakadu's mostly low-lying land is dominated by the flood plains of the East, South and West Alligator rivers, and flora such as rainforest plants, pandanus and paperbarks, as well as mangroves on the salty tidal flats thrive in this watery environment. This region has always supported correspondingly rich animal life, and the fish, birds, reptiles and mammals hunted by Aboriginal people for thousands of years are still abundant here.

Below Kakadu National Park contains some of the Australian continent's most important Aboriginal art sites, including the beautiful and fascinating 'galleries' of Ubirr Rock. These paintings, among the oldest in Australia and, indeed, the world, feature stick-like 'Mimi' figures – small, delicately formed spirits that the ancient Aborigines believed lived in and around the rocks of the Kakadu region. Although the national park also features really superb scenery and wildlife, its 1981 World Heritage listing is largely due to the presence of these internationally significant prehistoric art sites.

The build-up to the wet season from October to December was known as *Gunumeleng*, and the ensuing 'Wet' was divided into two phases: the monsoon time, or *Gudjewg*, and the storm time of *Bang-gereng*.

This tropical seasonality meant that food was scarce at certain times and plentiful at others and the people migrated, according to the season, from the high escarpment's dry rock shelters to the swamps and rivers of the flood plain. During these migration times it was common to travel up to 10km (6 miles) a day, and men hunting alone for fish, mammals and birds could walk up to 30km (19 miles) daily. Important food sources included magpie geese (both birds and eggs) and turtles from the swamps, and the women collected berries, fruit and tubers.

Some of Australia's most elaborate Aboriginal rock art galleries are found in Kakadu, with famous sites such as Ubirr and Nourlangie rocks exhibiting fine examples of the evolution of various art styles.

Aborigines of the Desert

Aboriginal life in the central deserts presented particular difficulties. Food was never abundant, water was always in short supply, and people moved about continuously, centring their lives on permanent water sources. Groups were always small, rarely more than 20 people, and a group's home country was vast. A major concentration of food was a rare event and so there was little opportunity for big gatherings. When these did occur, they were associated with unusually heavy rains which brought on a flush of food. Men hunted kangaroos, goannas and birds with spears, non-returning boomerangs and clubs, but contributed towards only a small amount of the daily food requirement.

The women collected seeds, fruit, insects and ants and, armed with detailed knowledge of over 100 species of desert plants and their fruiting cycles, were able to supply the day's food needs of the entire group in the space of just a few hours.

Women transported their bounty in wooden bowls balanced carefully on their heads, and 'hunted' food with heavy digging sticks. This indispensable tool was used to harvest a rich and unlikely food source, available a metre or two below the arid central Australian mulga (a small acacia tree): the honey-ant. The honey-ant collects honey to feed its young, and is highly prized as a

special delicacy. Aboriginal women still dig up the ants from their nests among the mulga roots. Kilograms of honey, enough to keep a group well fed for the whole day, can be obtained from a morning's digging.

Many of the region's rock shelters were, and in some places continue to be, decorated with paints made from

ochre and ash. Some painting sites depict hunts, journeys and other day-to-day matters, but others have deep spiritual significance. These sites, such as those at Uluru, are now strictly protected by both Aboriginal and non-Aboriginal law.

Aborigines in various parts of the Australian continent had, and continue to have, distinctive lifestyles and traditions. Although many Aboriginal people are now actively preserving their rich traditional beliefs and customs, no part of the continent remains untouched by the modern world and links with traditional lifestyles have all but disappeared in some urban Aboriginal communities. In all cases, however, there is a powerful desire to mix the old with the new and create distinctly modern identities for today's Aboriginal people.

The advent of Europeans to the continent in 1788 brought, among many other things, the beginning of the misrepresentation of how Aboriginal occupation had affected the land. A fundamental but incorrect European perception of Aboriginal Australia is that the Aborigines were, to use a much-quoted phrase, an 'unchanging

Above As their ancestors did for many thousands of years, these Aboriginal women in Queensland are gathering seeds for food. Traditionally the women always collect the bulk of the daily food requirement, supplementing plants with ants, grubs and other insects that are dug out of the ground.

Left Living off the land in the arid central deserts appeared to be an impossibility to early European explorers, but Aboriginal people saw the situation very differently. Their resourcefulness meant that plants, mammals, birds, insects and reptiles could all be turned into nutritious food. Although these goannas might look unappealing to many, they represent a tasty and highly sought-after meal to Aborigines.

Right Fires in the dry Australian bush have long been both a natural phenomenon and one that Aboriginal people encouraged to clear land and increase their food supply. Although devastation appears to be the immediate effect of a bushfire, Australia's extraordinary indigenous plant life regenerates remarkably quickly after these incidents. For some plants fire is a blessing – the unique grasstree, or xanthorrhoea, for example, flowers after fire and the tree's sturdy structure and composition make it highly fire-resistant. Many eucalypts have heat-resistant bark, and plants such as banksias and casuarinas produce seeds that lie dormant in the soil until fire leads them to germinate, creating rapid new growth.

Below Gold was discovered at Pine Creek in the Northern Territory in 1872, leading to an influx of prospectors to this isolated Overland Telegraph Line station. The men and equipment originally made the 230km (143 miles) journey to and from Darwin by track, but by the mid-1880s a railway line had been constructed – built largely with cheap Chinese labour. At one stage, Pine Creek's Chinese population outnumbered Europeans by 15 to one.

people in an unchanging land'. This precept, of course, is not true – the land has altered quite considerably over the millenia and the Aboriginal people have changed over the centuries. Even more importantly, the indigenous people of Australia affected the land and also its wildlife population and it is now clear that hunting and the use of fire had a profound impact on the landscape. Aborigines may even have played a part in the extinction of Australia's giant marsupials around 20 000 years ago.

When people refer to a 'natural' Australian landscape, they generally mean one which predated European arrival, but this pristine environment could only have existed in pre-Aboriginal Australia. The character of such a landscape is, anyway, now purely a matter of conjecture.

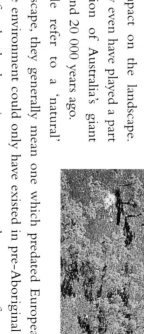

A RELUCTANT COLONY: AUSTRALIA'S EUROPEAN SETTLEMENT

The European colonisation of Australia is an improbable tale. The first and mostly reluctant 'pioneers' sent from Britain in 11 ships by King George in 1788 were a mixture of 1030 convicts, free settlers and military escorts: the 759 male and female convicts included professional and amateur thieves, prostitutes and military personnel who had offended their masters. An unlikely band to start a new nation!

The new colony was established by Captain Arthur Phillip who became the first governor at Sydney Cove, and within a decade this tiny port had become a focus for south sea trade, including exports such as seal and whale products. Gradually, thousands more settlers and convicts arrived and new convict settlements were established in Queensland, Tasmania and Western Australia. Convict transportation to New South Wales was abandoned in 1840, but the 1850s discovery of gold in New South Wales and other parts of the country led to a massive increase in migration. In addition to English, Scottish and Irish settlers, migrants arrived from China, Germany, the USA and many other parts of the globe.

The Chinese people, in particular, came to Australia looking for gold and they were found on goldfields anywhere from the Snowy Mountains of New South Wales to Pine Creek in the Northern Territory. A Victorian population census in 1857 revealed that there were 25 424 people of Chinese birth living in the state, only three of whom were women! The goldfields were often desperate places and on occasions racial tensions ran hot – for example, an ugly anti-Chinese riot broke out in 1861 at Young, in New South Wales. Nevertheless, the Australian diggings were regarded as relatively orderly places compared with the lawless contemporary rushes on other continents.

Left The 1850s discovery of rich gold resources in Victoria led to enormous growth in both the state's economy and its population. Melbourne, the Victorian capital, became wealthy and influential and rivalled Sydney for the honour of being the nation's premier city. The 1870s and 1880s boom period saw many grand buildings spring up around the city – including the vast domed Royal Exhibition Building, constructed to house the Great Melbourne Exhibition of 1880–81.

Below Built during the illustrious 1880s, when the city was known as 'Marvellous Melbourne', the ornate Princess Theatre is one of Melbourne's most famous Victorian buildings. This structure is the city's oldest surviving theatre and it still functions as a major performance space. Careful restoration in the late 1980s has brought the building, with its dome, ornate plasterwork, famous trumpeting angel and elegant interior, back to its former glory.

The 1850s and 1860s gold rushes made several strong impacts on the emerging nation. First, gold brought economic wealth – a fact which is still apparent in southern Australia's many fine late 19th-century buildings. Secondly, the enormous value of the gold found in Victoria established Melbourne as a settlement of comparable power and influence to that of the 'first city' of Sydney. This power struggle between the two cities, and the states of Victoria and New South Wales, still applies today. Another factor was the camaraderie of the diggers on the goldfields. This early 'mateship' can be regarded as the basis of the typically Australian egalitarian, anti-establishment personality. The subsequent 19th-century battles to establish trade unions, provide universal suffrage and challenge the power of central government and other authorities had part of their evolution on the diggings. Finally, the anti-Asian goldfields conflicts were the unfortunate beginnings of a racist 'White Australia' philosophy which persisted officially for well over a century.

By the end of the 19th century, the Australian colonies were exporting large quantities of gold and wool, almost entirely to Great Britain, and were paying their way in the world. In 1901 Australia became a self-governed federation, which combined all of the previously separate colonies. The remarkable foresight of the founding fathers of the Commonwealth of Australia is to be admired: even with modern communications, such a task of consolidation would be difficult today. New Zealand, then also a British colony, came close to being the seventh state of the Commonwealth but pulled out of the final referendum ballot. Nevertheless, the links between the two countries have always been strong. The World War I Australian and New Zealand Army Corps (ANZACs), for example, established a proud cross-Tasman tradition and provided the first major international identities for the two fledgling nations.

Australia has now established a strong identity and place in the world. The nation's cultural horizons changed dramatically in the 1950s and 1960s with the great immigrations from non-English-speaking Europe, particularly Italy and Greece. Melbourne is said to contain, after Athens and Thessaloniki, the world's third-largest Greek population. More recent 'new Australians' have included thousands of people from the Middle East and South-East Asia and, as a consequence of these migrations, the nature of Australian cities has changed radically. At one level these changes – in the availability of exotic cuisines, for example – are superficial, but many impacts have been far more profound. Multicultural influences have altered and broadened Australians' views of both the world and themselves.

One of the most powerful movements of the late 20th century has been the push to protect the natural environment on Australian farms. As the country grew and developed, the impact of 'progress' left a tragic legacy on the landscape. The grazing of 26 million cattle and 150 million sheep, and the cultivation of 20 million acres of land, created terrible problems. Native vegetation removal, soil erosion, damaged water tables and the introduction of exotic pests have all had serious impacts on the land and its ecosystems. A national 'Landcare' program, which aims to stabilise and even reverse two centuries of damage, has the wide support of rural people and is now a model program for rural areas throughout the world.

As the 20th century draws to a close, Australia's population has exceeded 18 million people and the continent is the breadbasket for many millions more. In addition to feeding itself well, the nation produces and exports vast quantities of mutton, beef, wheat, barley, sugar, fruit, fish and dairy products to the rest of the world.

At the beginning of the century, Australia was a group of English colonies, perched somewhat uncomfortably on the edge of Asia and completely dependent on Great Britain for cultural, economic and defence needs. It was a place where a 'whites only' policy of immigration was the norm and its Aboriginal people did not officially exist. But Australia can now look with pride at itself. Its melding of the old and new, also reflected in today's truly multicultural population, makes Australia both magnificent and distinctive. Its ancient contrasting landscapes and unique wildlife and flora mingle with its modern feats – such as the Snowy Mountains Hydro-Electric Scheme which pumps water to the dry interior, its man-made icons like the Sydney Harbour Bridge, Sydney Opera House, and Canberra's new Parliament House – to create a land of wonderful colour and great diversity.

Above Since its tentative beginnings in the middle of the 19th century, the cattle industry has occupied vast areas of Queensland, Western Australia and the Northern Territory, and coped with heat, dust, disease and incredible hardship. Australia's outback history is peppered with incredible tales of cattle droves, including the epic 1883–85 trek by the Durack family from Queensland to the north of Western Australia, with 7000 head of cattle.

Right Sheep were first introduced into Australia by the European settlers in 1788 and have become one of the continent's largest industries. Merinos, descended from a breed in Spain, make up nearly 75 per cent of the sheep population. In the five years preceding 1987, Australia produced 55 per cent of the world's merino wool, which amounts to about half of the total volume of wool sold in international markets.

The NORTH

THE TOP END: ARID AND TROPICAL

To most Australians the continent's far north, well beyond the Tropic of Capricorn, is a remote and wild world. The climate is monsoonal, generally divided into the 'Wet' (the hot, rainy period from October/November to March/April) and the 'Dry' (the still hot but less humid other months), and the rainfall is intense. Kakadu National Park receives an average of 1400mm (55in) of rain each year and devastating summer cyclones and washed-out roads are hazards for much of the region. But the remoteness, the abundance of wildlife and amazing plants and the extraordinary colours of the landscape are what makes this area, affectionately known as the Top End, so unique and special.

Lying close to Asia, the north has also been the continent's 'front door'. It is believed that Aboriginal people came to Australia from south-east or eastern Asia over 40 000 years ago via this coast. The Top End is still home to most of Australia's indigenous people and is rich in remnants of their ancestral culture.

The Northern Territory's lovely Kakadu National Park – Australia's largest – is the perfect place in which to understand something of Aboriginal life. This World Heritage reserve of sandstone escarpments, waterfalls, rivers and wetlands has been home to the Aborigines for at least 25 000 years. Evidence of their occupation is found in the vivid 'X-ray'-style paintings of Ubirr Rock and the colourful murals of Nourlangie Rock. Appropriately, Kakadu National Park is now under the custodianship of the local Aboriginal people.

The wildlife in this park is spectacular. Both crocodile species, the harmless freshwater and estuarine, are found in Kakadu, as are other reptiles such as snakes and goannas, and many exotic fish species. Dingoes and water buffalo roam the plains, and there is an amazing array of birdlife – including jabirus, brolgas and pelicans – around the wetlands formed by the flood plain of the three Alligator rivers. Controversially, uranium is mined here, extracted from the Ranger site near the town of Jabiru.

Kakadu National Park is bordered by the Arnhem Land escarpment, which runs for 600km (373 miles). Arnhem Land is an Aboriginal reserve and access is restricted, but tourists can visit Gurig National Park. The only significant European presence is on the Gove Peninsula, where bauxite is mined, and in the Gulf of Carpentaria at Groote Eylandt's manganese mines.

The Aboriginal-art-lined gorges, rainforest and birds of the Nitmiluk (Katherine Gorge) National Park are spectacular, as are the 500 million-year-old limestone caverns and formations of nearby Cutta Cutta. Elsey National Park takes in almost 14 000ha (43 594 acres) of the Roper River's headwaters and contains lush rainforest around the warm waters of Mataranka's thermal pool. Further north, Litchfield National Park is a splendid environment of cascading waterfalls, strange sandstone formations and tall termite mounds.

Left The extraordinary weathered shapes and contours of the Bungle Bungle massif are reflected in water after a rare period of rainfall. Located in Western Australia's arid far north, hundreds of these ancient beehive-shaped sandstone hills dot the otherwise flat landscape and form a unique natural wonder. Although Aborigines knew of their existence, the Bungle Bungles came to general attention only in the early 1980s.

Previous pages Boab trees are seen all over the Kimberley region in the north of Western Australia and the 'Top End' of the Northern Territory. These curious plants, one of Australia's few native deciduous trees, have bottle-shaped trunks which become grotesquely swollen, and often hollow, when the trees mature. This scene near Derby also shows large termite mounds, another common feature of Australia's far north.

Above In east Kimberley the vast man-made Lake Argyle, created as part of an irrigation scheme, provides a rare expanse of water.

Left The rugged coast of far north Western Australia, beyond Derby and around King Sound and the Buccaneer Archipelago, is one of the continent's most isolated regions.

Left A monsoonal climate means that Kakadu's river flood plains are transformed into extensive wetlands in summer, forming a sanctuary for many thousands of waterbirds.

Below This scene in Kakadu National Park reveals the beauty of the area's waterways, such as the Yellow Water billabong, or waterhole.

Port Darwin was named in honour of Charles Darwin and after many failed attempts the town flourished with the discovery of gold in this northern region in the 1870s. Darwin is now a melting pot of 76 000 people comprising some 45 different ethnic groups. The vagaries of its tropical location have often made life in Darwin very difficult. Its chequered history includes bombing by the Japanese during World War II and devastation by Cyclone Tracy in 1974. Appropriately, this multicultural city looks north towards Asia, across the Timor and Arafura seas. Between Darwin and Indonesia lie Bathurst and Melville islands, home to the Tiwi people, whose isolation from the mainland has created a distinct Aboriginal language and culture from that of Aborigines on the mainland.

Most of the Territory's northern towns grew up around the cattle industry and the 1870s Overland Telegraph Line. Katherine, Daly Waters and Pine Creek all began life while the

telegraph line was being laid. Pine Creek also started thriving after its 1872 gold rush, which brought prospectors of many nationalities to the previously isolated region.

From Katherine, the Victoria Highway makes its lonely way towards the Western Australian border. This sparsely populated region contains the Keep River and Gregory national parks with their cave paintings, rivers and spectacular gorges. Nearby Victoria River Downs was once the world's largest cattle station at an incredible 30 000km² (11 580 sq miles), while to the south lie Aboriginal lands and the desolate Tanami Desert.

The Victoria Highway leads west to the town of Kununurra just across the Western Australian border and the vast, beautiful, isolated area known as Kimberley. It is a land of wild coastline, magnificent sandstone formations, limestone gorges, rivers, and cattle stations and it is rich in Aboriginal history. Modern Kununurra, built as the centre for the Ord River

Irrigation Scheme of the 1960s and 1970s, provides a striking contrast to the extended indigenous occupation of the area. Centred on Lake Argyle, Australia's largest man-made waterway, the scheme irrigates vast tracts of agricultural land. Further to the south, Australia's only diamond mine, the Argyle Diamond Mine, produces highly prized white, champagne and even pink gemstones.

There are several national parks on the Kimberley plateau. By far the most spectacular is Purnululu (Bungle Bungle) National Park with its famous layered towers of rock. These fragile, beehive-shaped hills and domes, up to 300m (984ft) high, are composed of 350 million-year-old sandstone. The Bungle Bungles were well frequented by the ancient Aboriginal peoples and there are several examples of their rock art, as well as their burial and sacred sites here. The Mirima (Hidden Valley) National Park is a similar environment that also features the region's curiously bloated boab (or baobab) trees. Limestone is predominant in Windjana Gorge and Geikie Gorge national parks – which embrace rivers, gorges, freshwater and estuarine crocodiles, rock wallabies, over 100 species of birds, and beautifully decorated caves and rock shelters.

The Kimberley's far north, bordering the Timor Sea, is a rarely visited region of nature reserves, island-dotted coastline and small Aboriginal settlements. It is also where the port of Wyndham is situated. Surrounded by the rivers and tidal mudflats of Cambridge Gulf, the far north supports estuarine crocodiles and prolific birdlife. To the south, the rugged King Leopold Ranges rise to 1000m (3281ft). Incredibly, a road crosses this inhospitable area: the

Above Australians are keen sports fans and hang-gliding is a must for adrenaline junkies. A different kind of high is the sport of bungy jumping. It involves leaping off the side of a tall structure with specially designed elasticised bands strapped around the ankles of the 'victim' to haul them back upwards before they hit the surface below.

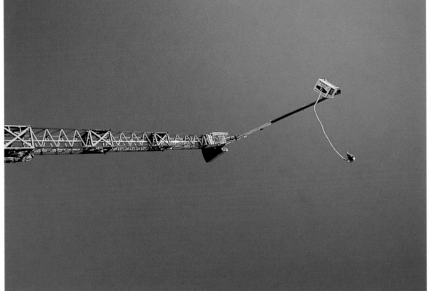

670km-long (416 miles) Gibb River Road, originally used to transport cattle, joins Wyndham with Derby in the west. On King Sound, an inlet with a tidal range of up to 12m (39ft), Derby is the administrative centre for a large cattle region and has an important Royal Flying Doctor Service base.

Further south on the coast, Broome, the Kimberley's largest town, was settled in the early 1870s when the presence of high-quality pearls brought Japanese and Asian pearlers to Roebuck Bay. A racially mixed town of around 6000 people, it has become the centre of a thriving tourist industry, catering for those drawn by the tropical climate, Indian Ocean beaches and sights such as Gantheaume Point's dinosaur footprints.

There are other settlements in the Kimberley region including the inland highway village of Fitzroy Crossing, which serves the local Aboriginal communities, and Halls Creek, the scene of a frantic 1880s gold rush. Halls Creek is at the end of the 1700km-long (1056 miles) Canning Stock Route, once used for cattle droving. To the south lie the central deserts and Wolfe Creek Crater – 850m (930yd) wide and 50m (164ft) deep – believed to have been formed by a meteorite plummeting to earth a million years ago.

The eastern Tropics present a marked contrast to the wild western Kimberley landscape. Queensland's long coastline and fertile hinterland are well populated and accessible, and the intricate Great Barrier Reef and offshore islands form Australia's most popular holiday playground. James Cook, one of Queensland's first 'tourists', damaged his ship while attempting to negotiate a passage through the reef in 1770. For seven weeks the ship was moored for repairs on the Cook River at the site of present-day Cooktown.

The Great Barrier Reef, its significance recognised by a World Heritage listing, stretches for 2300km (1429 miles) from Lady Elliot Island near the Tropic of Capricorn to the Gulf of Papua north of Cape York. This wonder of the world is

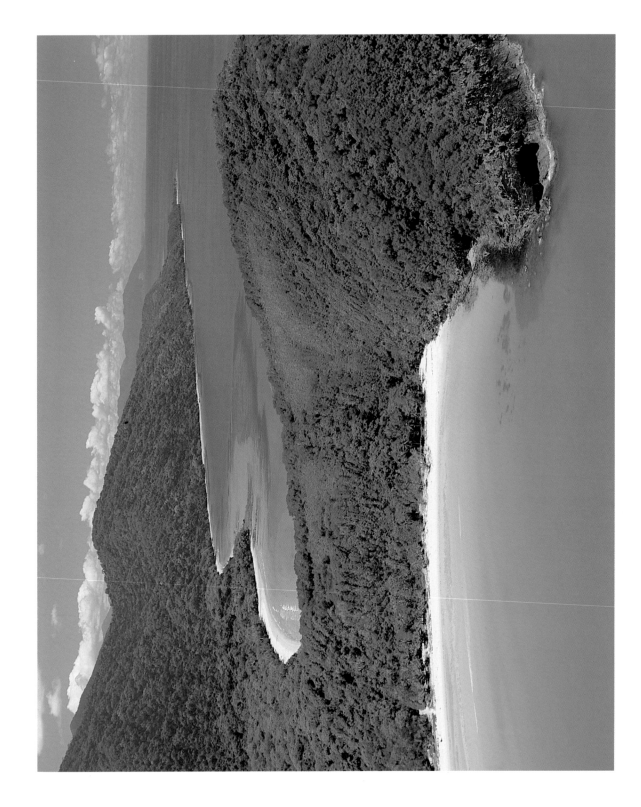

Above In Queensland's north-east, lush rainforest spills down the hillsides, almost to the water's edge, to create a most unusual landscape. This scene, in the exquisite Cape Tribulation National Park, reveals a striking contrast between the dense vegetation and white sandy beaches lapped by the Coral Sea's crystal-clear waters.

actually a series of over 2000 separate reefs combined with islands and their fringing reefs. Created by algae and the skeletons of tiny coral polyps, this living, growing reef varies in width from 15km (9 miles) in the north to 300km (186 miles) further south. The fantastic world of colourful and strangely shaped corals is also home to 1500 species of fish, turtles, manta rays, dugongs (sea cows) and whales, as well as more dangerous sharks, sea snakes and box jellyfish. The structure's fragility is of great concern, however, as crown-of-thorns starfish eat their way through the coral and fishing, tourism and shipping all leave their mark on this unique environment.

Despite the presence of the reef and its coral cays – such as Green Island and the turtle nesting site of Heron Island – most of Queensland's islands are continental. That is, the 100 or so Whitsunday Islands were once part of a coastal range that became separated from the mainland after post-Ice Age flooding. They are now a paradise of birdlife, forested hills, white beaches and startlingly blue waters. These islands, close to Proserpine's sugarcane-growing region, include several national parks. Australia's largest island park, Hinchinbrook,

is dominated by high jagged peaks, abundant rainforest, birds such as herons and kingfishers, and goannas. The northern resort islands include rainforested Dunk Island, Fitzroy Island and Lizard Island, well beyond Cooktown.

From the cattle town of Rockhampton north of the Tropic of Capricorn, the fertile Queensland coast stretches northwards to the tip of Cape York Peninsula and encompasses many coastal and inland national parks. With a population of 96 000, Townsville on the north-east coast is Australia's largest tropical city. Founded in the 1860s on the cattle industry and now a major port and tourism centre, it is an excellent point for visiting the reef and Magnetic Island – part national park and home to cockatoos, goannas, koalas and wallabies. Further north, the well-watered Ingham–Innisfail region grows vast

quantities of sugarcane and tropical fruits. Cairns, originally a goldfields port, is now the hub of northern Queensland's booming tourist industry. The 'Marlin Coast' to the city's north has some excellent beaches although, in addition to its famous game fish, this Coral Sea coastline is home to the poisonous box jellyfish, making summer swimming hazardous.

The fertile Queensland Tropics contain Australia's wettest place – Mount Bellenden Ker in the Bellenden Ker National Park – where a drenching 11 250mm (443in) of rain fell during 1979. Beyond the tourist centre of Port Douglas, the 'Queensland Wet Tropics' form another World Heritage area. Including Daintree and Cape Tribulation national parks, this is a magical world of dense rainforest, rivers, deep gorges, sandy beaches and the world's highest concentration of flowering plants. The wildlife here includes crocodiles, colourful butterflies, snakes, the flightless cassowary and Bennett's tree kangaroo, a species that is unique to the area.

Tropical Queensland's interior also takes in the Atherton Tableland, an upland farming region of volcanic craters, lakes and exotic rainforest; the caves and ridges of the dry limestone Chillagoe–Mungana National Park; and the strange Undara underground lava-tube, believed to be the longest system in the world. These tubes are remnants of an eruption some 19 000 years ago. Mineral riches abound here too. In the 1870s gold was found at the remote Palmer River, inland from Cooktown, and around the cattle city of Charters Towers, while towns such as Mount Garnet, Anakie and Moura have thrived on mining copper, tin, gold, coal and sapphires.

Further north, Cape York Peninsula's pristine beauty, ranging from coastal mangroves to rainforest and interior waterways, has been conserved in 10 national parks. The fauna here includes crocodiles and rich birdlife, while barramundi inhabit the Gulf of Carpentaria and the Coral Sea. Settlements are few – the bauxite mining town of Weipa, isolated cattle stations and Aboriginal communities – but Cape York's indigenous people have left a spectacular mark at Quinkan Reserve, one of the world's largest prehistoric art sites. Beyond the Cape's tip, the Torres Strait Islands are home to substantial numbers of people of Aboriginal, Papuan and Asian origin, who make a living from pearling and fishing.

To the south-west, the flood plains of the 'Gulf Country' contain cattle-farming towns and prawn or barramundi fishing towns such as Karumba and Normanton. The highlights of this Gulf of Carpentaria region, however, are Lawn Hill National Park, with its verdant rainforest, sandstone gorges and Aboriginal art sites; and also the globally significant Riversleigh World Heritage fossil site, where the remains of many prehistoric animals have been found.

Despite its remoteness from the south, Australia's north has long received foreign 'visitors' – from the first Aborigines to 15th-century Macassan (Indonesian) fishermen who came for sea cucumbers to European explorers such as Abel Tasman. In modern times the north has been regarded as Australia's most vulnerable region – it was bombed during World War II, encroached on by boat people from Vietnam, and now the domain of the most recent bombardment: tourists.

Below With its forested hills, beautiful beaches and sheltered waters, the Whitsunday coast and islands are among Australia's most popular holiday destinations. Located around the town of Airlie Beach and the nearby village of Shute Harbour, this central Queensland region offers sailing, boating, snorkelling, scuba diving and bushwalking – there are over 100 islands, and the Great Barrier Reef is within easy reach. Like many places along the east coast, this region was named by Captain James Cook, who passed by here on Whitsunday in June 1770.

Below Unlike many of Queensland's islands, Green Island, off the major northern settlement of Cairns, is a true coral cay. Located right on the Great Barrier Reef, rainforest-covered Green Island is a national park, but also the home of a resort and an underwater observatory. The 13ha (32 acres) cay is surrounded by colourful coral and a wonderful variety of marine life – from tiny, bright-hued reef fish to clams, starfish and sharks. This area is also an important nesting site for seabirds, which flock to nearby Michaelmas Cay each summer.

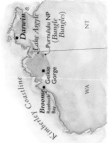

West Kimberley

Above In the far north of Western Australia, Broome is the gateway to the spectacular Kimberley region – a land of rivers, gorges, mountain ranges and ancient rocks that has changed little for many thousands of years. Founded in the 1870s as a pearling centre, Broome is a relaxed tropical town of around 11 000 people. The presence of the fine pearls brought many Asian merchants and divers to Broome, and by the early 1900s, the town had become the world's pearling capital. This industry continues, and the area's exquisite cultured pearls are highly prized. The region is famous for its pristine beaches and craggy rock formations, and is becoming increasingly popular as a tourist destination.

Right Located on Roebuck Bay (named after the Roebuck, on which the adventurer William Dampier explored this coast in the late 1600s), Broome is surrounded by clear turquoise-coloured waters and long stretches of white beaches. The heavily eroded reddish-orange rocks around these beaches contain fascinating archaeological remnants in the form of dinosaur footprints, believed to be the marks of a large reptile that lived around 120 million years ago.

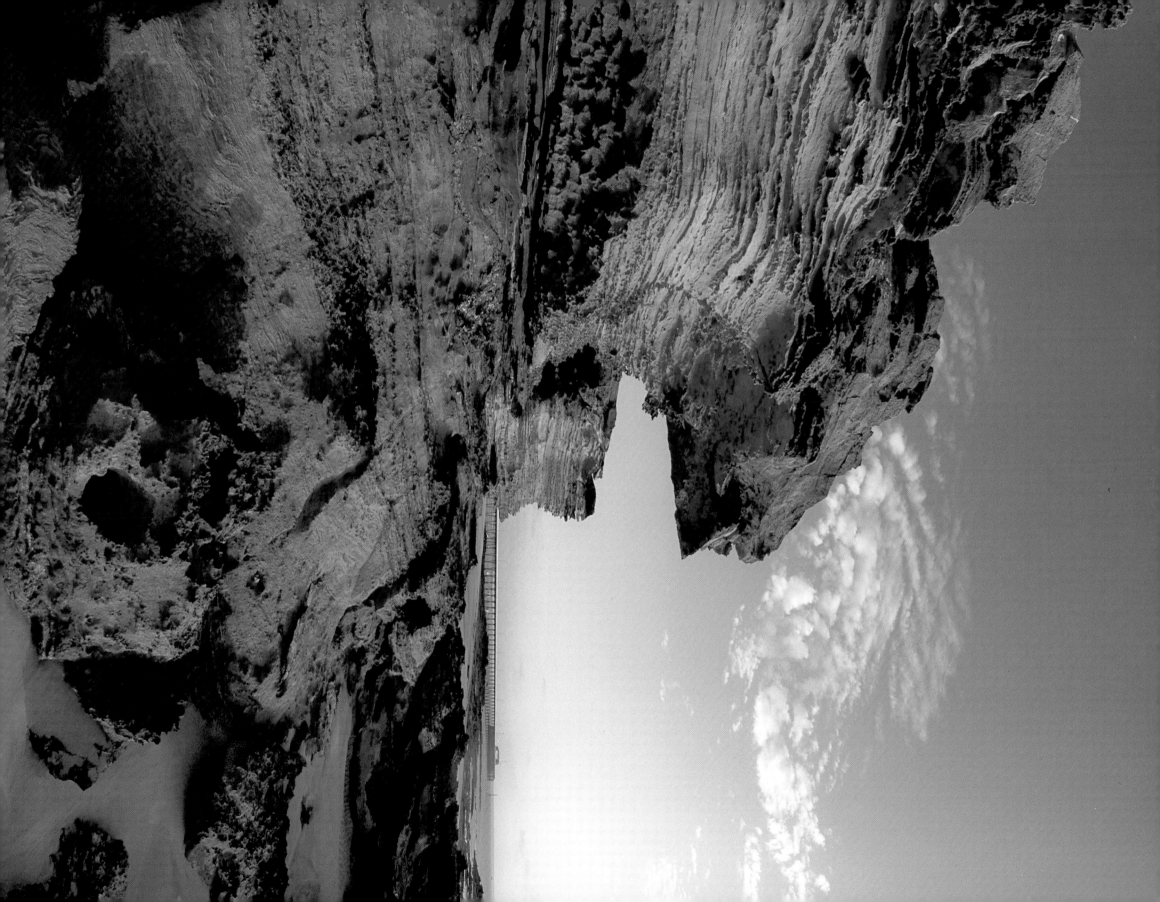

The Broome coastline

Above To the south of Broome, the coastline stretches in a broad arc towards the major settlement of Port Hedland, which is reputed to be Western Australia's fastest-growing town. The beaches here are remote and all but deserted and, other than isolated farms and cattle stations, there is very little sign of habitation in the area. The lonely Great Northern Highway follows the coast's contours, with just the occasional roadhouse to break the monotony of the vast flat plains. This beach and its craggy rocks are at Barn Hill, which is south of Broome and located between capes Gourdon and Villaret.

Right Although it is very rarely visited, this remote coast features some very striking scenery. As this spectacular aerial view of the Pindan region, also to the south of Broome, reveals, the extremely flat and low-lying plain terminates abruptly, falling to the beach in the form of sheer, heavily weathered red cliffs. The scrub-covered plain stretches far into the distance and it ultimately becomes the vast and extremely barren Great Sandy Desert. The Great Sandy Desert covers an enormous area of Western Australia's arid north, about the size of both Italy and Britain combined.

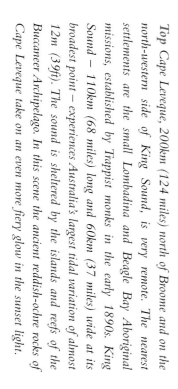

Top Cape Leveque, 200km (124 miles) north of Broome and on the north-western side of King Sound, is very remote. The nearest settlements are the small Lombadina and Beagle Bay Aboriginal missions, established by Trappist monks in the early 1890s. King Sound – 110km (68 miles) long and 60km (37 miles) wide at its broadest point – experiences Australia's largest tidal variation of almost 12m (39ft). The sound is sheltered by the islands and reefs of the Buccaneer Archipelago. In this scene the ancient reddish-ochre rocks of Cape Leveque take on an even more fiery glow in the sunset light.

Purnululu (Bungle Bungle) National Park

Left Rising abruptly from the arid East Kimberley plains, the deep-red, brown and ochre-striped Bungle Bungles are indeed a spectacular sight. These curiously named sandstone formations reach a height of 300m (984ft) and cover a large area that has been protected within the 3000km² (1158 sq miles) Purnululu (an Aboriginal word meaning sandstone) National Park since 1987. Visitors are welcome here, but access and numbers are strictly controlled to preserve this extremely delicate environment. The 350 million-year-old sandstone, itself a very friable substance, is coated with a fragile layer of silica and lichen that protects the rock from rain and the more severe forms of erosion — a vital necessity if this extraordinary natural wonder is to be protected.

Although most of this East Kimberley region is semidesert, a surprising range of vegetation grows in the national park, including hardy eucalypts and the lush and unique Bungle Bungle fan palms, in addition to the ubiquitous spinifex and other drought-resistant shrubs and grasses in the more open areas. It would take days or even weeks to explore the canyons, gorges and valleys of the park, so most visitors head for a couple of special sites. Magical Cathedral Gorge is a large natural amphitheatre at the end of a narrow ravine, while Picaninny Creek offers particularly unusual rock formations, sheer rock walls and a collection of the area's delightful fan palms.

Above left It is not surprising that such a dominating landform and powerful 'presence' as the Bungle Bungles features prominently in Aboriginal life, and the area has always been of great significance to the local indigenous people. The maze of overhangs and canyons here once provided shelter for these nomadic people, and Purnululu contains dozens of rock art locations, as well as a number of burial areas and sacred sites. Other long-time inhabitants of these rocks and gorges are the ever present birds, reptiles and mammals, such as magnificent wedge-tailed eagles, snakes and goannas, and rock wallabies.

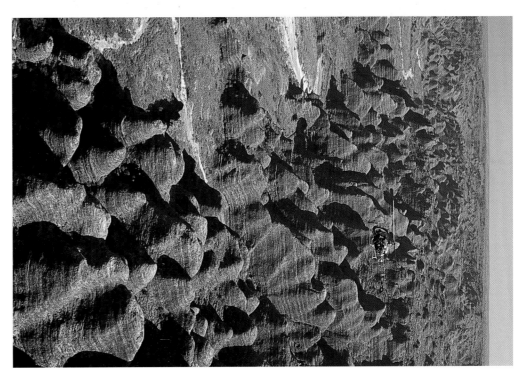

Above right Tour groups and independent visitors can explore the Bungle Bungles — but only with sturdy four-wheel-drive vehicles — by driving along the authorised tracks. The really adventurous can even bushwalk and camp here at a couple of designated sites for a very special wilderness experience. The driving tracks, however, are extremely rugged and the park is closed during the summer wet season when these trails are frequently flooded. Overall, viewing the region from the air is a much more spectacular and environmentally sensitive option, and there are several operators in the nearby towns of Halls Creek and Kununurra who offer aeroplane and helicopter tours for a bird's eye view of this distinctive natural wonder.

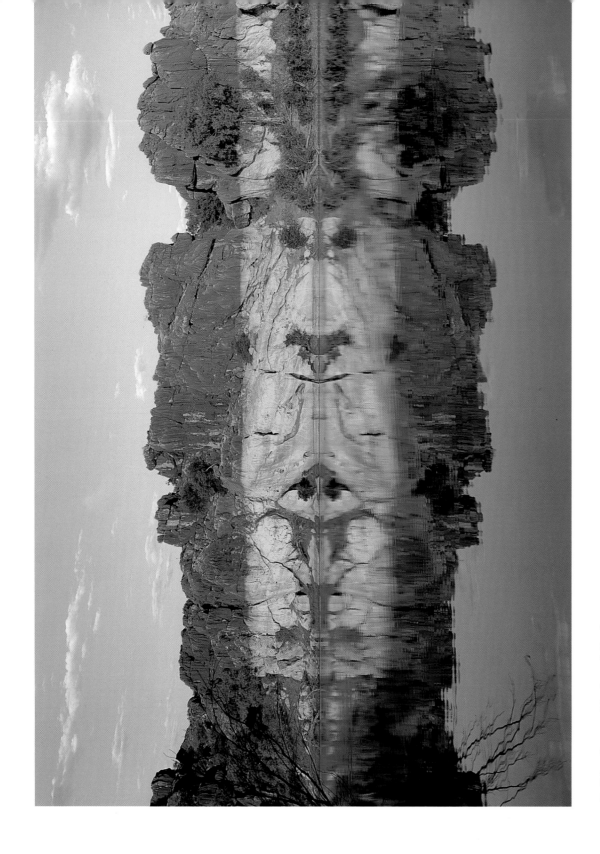

Geikie Gorge National Park

Above Formed by the waters of the mighty Fitzroy River, which flows for over 600km (373 miles) and enters the sea at King Sound north of Derby, dramatic Geikie Gorge is a highlight of the West Kimberley. Contained within a 3000ha (7413 acres) national park, this 14km-long (9 miles) gorge features 30–50m-high (98–164ft) walls that are banded in subtle colours. The river is home to stingrays, fish such as barramundi and sawfish, and crocodiles. These, however, are not the man-eating estuarine variety but the smaller freshwater or Johnston's 'croc', which prefers to prey on fish and small animals.

Below left and right Located a few kilometres from the tiny Great Northern Highway town of Fitzroy Crossing, Geikie Gorge National Park is open to visitors only between the cooler and drier months of April and October. In the summer wet season, the Fitzroy River swells to a raging torrent and floods the surrounding countryside, making the gorge and national park off-limits. The gorge is the result of the river slowly cutting its way through an ancient coral reef that once enclosed a shallow sea – the deeply weathered cliff faces here contain a remarkable array of marine fossils that include fish, corals and shells.

Below Geikie Gorge's cliffs bear a marked difference in their bands of colour, the reddish-brown of the gorge's upper level contrasting strongly with the bleached-looking rock below. The pale colour of the gorge's lower wall is the result of regular flood action that has scoured the rock and exposed the intriguing fossil deposits. When the flood waters recede, the river drops by as much as 16m (53ft), which leaves only sandbanks interspersed with large waterholes in particularly dry periods. The best way to study the gorge walls is by boat, an option taken by most of the park's visitors, or even from the air for a truly panoramic view.

Below The remote Kimberley has always been one of the continent's most important and traditional Aboriginal regions, and there is a substantial indigenous population here today. Many of these people are involved in the cattle and tourism industries, and this region and its national park increasingly offer the local skills and knowledge of Aboriginal rangers and guides. Operators in the Kimberley area run Aboriginal-themed tours, including an illuminating cruise through the Geikie Gorge National Park which reveals many of the secrets of its 350 million-year-old walls.

Emma Gorge

Above Located on the 400 000ha (988 400 acres) El Questro Station in the East Kimberley, Emma Gorge is a delightful region of sheer rock walls, shady canyons and wet season waterfalls. Surrounded by rivers and the high Cockburn, Pentecost and Durack ranges, this station is a working cattle property, but visitors can stay at the homestead or resort and explore the area's many gorges, springs and thermal pools. Also on the station is the dramatic, narrow El Questro Gorge with its 60m-high (197ft) walls separated by only a few metres. El Questro is reached via the rough Gibb River Road, which runs for about 670km (416 miles) from Derby on the west coast to Kununurra, and which was built to transport cattle from remote stations to the area's ports.

King George Falls

Right In the East Kimberley's extremely remote far north, the King George River makes its way from its source in the Drysdale River National Park to the Timor Sea. From this inland region of rugged ranges, escarpments and a high plateau, the river cascades 60m (197ft) over heavily eroded red cliffs, as seen here at King George Falls, before it continues north to spill into the tropical sea. This ancient, sparsely vegetated landscape has been little touched by man – the only settlements here are isolated cattle stations, and the Aboriginal town of Kalumburu. Even the national park, one of the most remote in Australia, has no road access and receives very few visitors other than scientists and the most dedicated bushwalkers and nature lovers.

East Kimberley

Left The miracle of irrigation has transformed a large area of the dry and rugged East Kimberley into highly fertile agricultural land. Most of the precious water comes from Lake Argyle – a vast man-made reservoir that forms the focus of the Ord River Irrigation Scheme. The main dam here was opened in 1972, halting the enormous flow of the Ord River that previously poured into the sea at Cambridge Gulf. The lake holds nine times the volume of water contained in Sydney Harbour and, despite its undoubted usefulness, the project created considerable controversy when it flooded an area containing ancient Aboriginal relics and sanctuaries for birds and other wildlife. Peanuts, soya beans, maize, sorghum and large amounts of exotic fruit (including melons, mangoes and bananas) are produced in this region and then transported over enormous distances to markets in Perth and other faraway cities.

Above In the remote northern reaches of the isolated East Kimberley, the settlement of Kalumburu is an Aboriginal reserve and mission town. Although few outsiders ever venture so far north, tourists can visit the area, but only with a pre-arranged permit. Well north of Drysdale River National Park, and at the end of a 250km-long (155 miles) dirt road that leads off the Great Northern Highway, Kalumburu's remoteness allows its Aboriginal inhabitants to live a relatively traditional life, far away from modern Western conventions and pressures.

Kakadu National Park

Previous pages Added to the World Heritage list in the 1980s, Kakadu's 20 000km² (7720 sq miles) form Australia's largest national park. This region of rivers, low-lying flood plains, rocky outcrops, water-falls, rainforest and woodland is backed by the magnificent buttress of the Arnhem Land escarpment that runs for 600km (373 miles) across the tropical 'Top End' of the Northern Territory. This is a remarkably varied environment where a wide range of fauna – including crocodiles, tree snakes, goannas, rock wallabies, dingoes and bats – thrives. The birdlife is prolific too, particularly around the wetlands. Aborigines inhabited Kakadu for at least 25 000 years – possibly for as long as 50 000 – and neighbouring Arnhem Land has been inhabited by a large number of Australia's indigenous people. Kakadu itself has been under the custodianship of its traditional owners for some years, but the park was leased to the National Parks and Wildlife Service in 1978.

Left Kakadu National Park's ancient Aboriginal art, most particularly that of the Ubirr and Nourlangie rock galleries, is deservedly world-famous and an important factor in the park's dual World Heritage listing for natural and cultural reasons.

These striking paintings are around 20 000 years old and rival the prehistoric sites of southern Europe in their archaeological importance. Depicted in natural ochres, reds and whites, Nourlangie Rock's murals feature fish, male and female figures, spirit beings and 'Namarkon', the mythical lightning man who is the spirit being responsible for thunder, lightning and storms. Most of these paintings are in the 'X-ray' style which, remarkably, depicts the subject's internal anatomical features.

Below Once used as a shelter and therefore frequented by the local people, Ubirr Rock forms a treasure-house of indigenous art. Shielded by an overhang which has helped to preserve the paintings, the main gallery contains some extraordinary work. Fish and figures from the spirit world are featured here, as well as humans, turtles, kangaroos and other animals. Ubirr Rock's murals also depict stick-like 'Mimi' spirits which, according to Aboriginal legend, live in these rocky caves and crevices. There are another 30 or so smaller art sites in the vicinity.

Nitmiluk (Katherine Gorge) National Park

Above Another of the Northern Territory's most famous attractions lies less than 100km (62 miles) south of Kakadu, in the Nitmiluk (Katherine Gorge) National Park. This is where the Katherine River has carved its way through a sandstone plateau and created not just one gorge, but a series of 13 stunning canyons that are separated by rapids. The 60m-high (197ft) ochre-coloured walls that turn a deep orange-red at dawn and dusk are covered with ancient Aboriginal paintings of human figures, crocodiles and other local fauna.

Right The best way to view the splendour of the Katherine Gorge region is by boat, and such tours take visitors along the river through several of the gorges. Many are inaccessible when water levels fall considerably during the dry season, and others can be reached only by canoe. The area is also great for walking, with over 100km (62 miles) of marked trails. Another highlight of Nitmiluk National Park is the delightful Edith Falls which tumble off the Arnhem Land escarpment into a cool, palm-fringed pool.

Litchfield National Park

Above Although much less well-known than its famous 'neighbour' Kakadu, Litchfield National Park, just 120km (75 miles) south-west of Darwin, offers some superb natural features and attractions. This is a region of rivers, waterfalls, monsoonal rainforest and a rugged sandstone plateau, while the northern section of the park contains many tall, wedge-shaped termite mounds. The termites live in colonies of many thousands and, like ants, divide their food-gathering, reproductive and defensive duties among workers, queens and soldiers.

Opposite top Varying in height and shape but dotted across the Litchfield landscape like curious gravestones, these tunnel-riddled mounds housing countless termite colonies have a fascinating common feature: the narrow sides all run in a north-south direction while the broad 'wedges' face east and west. This has led to the structures being termed 'magnetic', but it actually represents a means of controlling the temperature within the mounds – by facing the thinnest edges north-south, the full heat of the day strikes the smallest possible area.

Right Litchfield's termite 'homes' are undoubtedly interesting, but there are other fascinating sights here. Rivalling the mounds in their upward thrust, the free-standing sandstone pillars of the 'Lost City' have been weathered to resemble craggy buildings and even people. This park is also known for its permanent waterfalls, such as the Florence and Wangi falls, which cascade off the escarpment into clear, palm-fringed pools. There are also many walking tracks in the park, many of which lead to lookouts and superb views of the rugged region.

Cape York Peninsula

Opposite The vast Cape York Peninsula is a particularly wild and remote corner of the continent. At 10°41' south, Cape York itself lies far within the tropics and the climate is hot and monsoonal. Although the peninsula has long been occupied by Aboriginal people, the first short-lived European attempt to inhabit this inhospitable area was made at Somerset in the far north in 1863. Today there are numerous Aboriginal settlements at places such as Kowanyama and at Bamaga, almost at the tip of the cape. The only large town is west-coast Weipa, which relies on bauxite mining. The first known European landing on the continent was made near this town in 1606, when the Dutch explorer Willem Jansz ventured ashore from his ship, the Duyfken.

Above The Cape York Peninsula includes a really great variety of scenery – from high craggy peaks to pockets of rainforest and coastal swampland. The peninsula's most precious environments are conserved within several national parks, including Lakefield (north of the Quinkan Reserve) and its extraordinary array of prehistoric rock paintings. This large reserve includes woodland as well as grassland, but it also takes in a mangrove-lined coast and river flood plains. It is crocodile territory for both the estuarine and freshwater species, and it is also a major bird habitat. A striking contrast is found within Cape Melville National Park, where the rugged granite mountains and cliffs feature a variety of caves and rocky headlands.

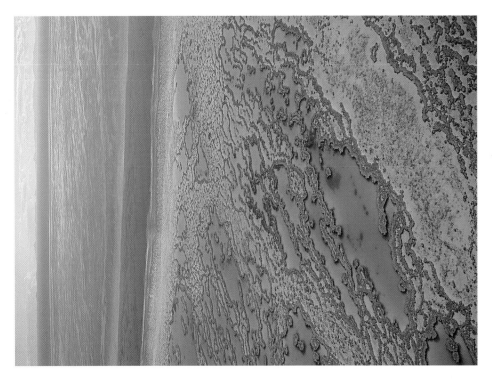

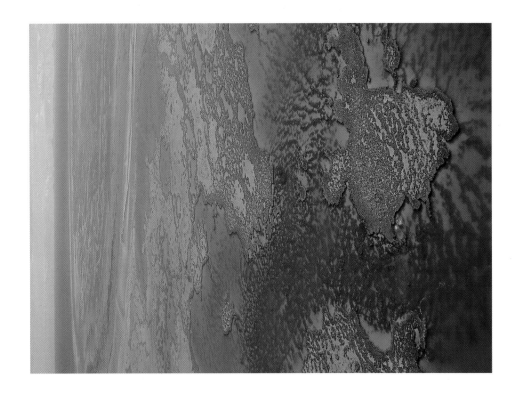

The Great Barrier Reef

Above and opposite Stretching for an amazing 2300km (1429 miles) off the Queensland coast – from the Gulf of Papua (north of Cape York) to offshore from the town of Gladstone (south of the Tropic of Capricorn) – the unique Great Barrier Reef naturally invites many descriptive superlatives. This is the planet's largest living structure, considered by many people to be the eighth wonder of the world, and it is the gem of the UNESCO World Heritage list – the reef is very special in that it fulfils all four of the body's natural heritage criteria.

Although known by a singular name, this remarkable structure is in fact composed of over 2000 separate but linked reefs, supplemented by many coral cays, islands and their fringing reefs. Created by tiny coral polyps, the limestone skeletons of which form the reef's basis, as well as algae and sands that bind the whole together, the Great Barrier Reef is an enormous living, growing structure that has evolved over hundreds of thousands of years. A huge coral reef such as this can only inhabit tropical waters, where the temperature does not fall below 20°C (68°F) and where other conditions,

such as a lack of sediments, are paramount. The Great Barrier Reef, unlike fringing reefs that hug the shoreline, is often a considerable distance from the coast – it is quite common to travel by boat for one to two hours from Queensland's coastal resorts to reach the reef.

In addition to its World Heritage status, the reef is under the protection of the Great Barrier Reef Marine Park which encompasses a vast area of ocean off the Queensland coast. Despite this, commercial fishing, scientific research and tourism are permitted here, although these activities are limited and strictly controlled. To really appreciate its extent, the Great Barrier Reef is best viewed from the air, when an extraordinary range of patterns and colours of sea and coral are revealed.

Left It is not difficult to see why the North Queensland coast is so popular with tourists. The idyllic weather and the fantastic coastal scenery are further enhanced by the proximity of the Great Barrier Reef. The reef provides a protective 'barrier', which means that the coastal waters are usually very calm and therefore perfect for sailing.

A magical underwater world

Opposite Other intriguing and colourful inhabitants of this unique underwater wonderland are the reef's corals. There is an incredible variety growing along the Great Barrier Reef – 350 species, ranging in colour from bluish-grey to yellow to red. They can be divided into two broad categories: true reef corals are the 'hard' or 'stony' type that actually build the reef – these include well-known formations such as 'brain' corals, with patterns that create the markings of a human brain, and 'staghorns' that protrude like the antlers of a deer. When the polyps that create these corals die, the formations lose their colour but remain as the white masses of calcium carbonate that are often seen washed up on Queensland's beaches.

The flexible, almost leathery, 'soft' corals, which include a delicate and commonly seen greenish-blue variety, have a more feathery look. This group also includes the more flamboyant 'branching' corals, which are distinguished by their elegant fern-like shapes and look more like plants as they wave about under the water.

Although this beautiful underwater world is best appreciated by scuba diving across its depths and mingling with the marine life, snorkelling also has its merits. Visitors who wish to stay dry are catered for, with glass-bottomed boats, semi-submersible craft and underwater observatories providing a glimpse of this incredible submarine fairyland.

Top, centre and bottom In looks really spectacular from the air, but the true magic of the Great Barrier Reef lies underneath the water's surface. This remarkable submarine world is an extraordinary environment of vibrant movement and colour, featuring around 1500 fish species, as well as sharks, turtles, manta rays and a variety of marine mammals. These impossibly colourful tropical reef fish – the almost luminous square-spot anthias (top), the bright red spine-cheek anemone fish (centre) and a giant Maori wrasse (bottom) – are just some of the many strange and fascinating creatures that cruise these Coral Sea and South Pacific waters.

Daintree and Cape Tribulation national parks

Above The *Queensland Wet Tropics World Heritage* region, which includes several areas around the north Queensland coast, is a unique environment of high rainfall, forested hills and an impossibly beautiful coastline. Inland and to the north of Port Douglas, the Daintree National Park forms a moist and verdant world of rainforest, ferns, mosses and an incredible variety of flowering plants, including many orchid species. Other integral elements of this densely vegetated eco-system are the many rivers, streams, gorges and waterfalls that all add up to an 'enchanted forest' atmosphere. Daintree inhabitants include crocodiles; huge, colourful birdwing butterflies; Australia's second largest bird, the flightless cassowary, which is not unlike the emu; and frogs and snakes. The Daintree has been World Heritage-listed since 1989.

Right Further north-east and on the coast, Cape Tribulation National Park presents a very different side of this Wet Tropics region. There are virtually impenetrable rainforests here too, but these peter out as the steep hillsides reach the water's edge. The beaches, interspersed with rocky headlands, are virtually deserted and the warm Coral Sea waters lap at their edges. Despite this idyllic picture, the area is crocodile territory, while jellyfish and other marine stingers make swimming a hazard, particularly during summer. Captain James Cook certainly had his doubts about this region, naming the cape so unflatteringly because his ship, the Endeavour, was damaged on a nearby reef in 1770.

Hinchinbrook Island

Left Australia's, and indeed the world's, largest national park island at 39 350ha (97 234 *acres*), Hinchinbrook Island lies off the town of Cardwell on the north Queensland coast. Capped by 1142m-high (3747ft) Mount Bowen, this island is the province of a chain of soaring eroded peaks, dense rainforest, mangrove swamps and deserted sandy beaches. There is only one low-key resort on the 37km-long (23 *miles*) island and relatively few visitors reach here – many of those that venture across the Hinchinbrook Channel come to camp in the national park, and to appreciate a very special wilderness environment. The channel itself contains excellent fishing grounds and the region supports a considerable bird population, including herons and kingfishers. Hinchinbrook also offers some very challenging walks, including a trek of five days or so along the wilderness of the island's east coast.

Above Hinchinbrook's east coast beaches are an unspoilt environment of golden sand and clear Coral Sea waters around which fossils, such as these interesting specimens, can be found. The beaches extend to the island's far north-east, where forest grows almost to the water's edge – eucalypts, including red gums and stringy-barks, thrive here. The forest is also home to sunbirds, kingfishers and a variety of other birds, while other Hinchinbrook wildlife includes goannas and green tree snakes.

Below Cardwell is one of the departure points for Hinchinbrook Island. This holiday centre features beaches, recreational fishing and inland forest drives. The high rainfall (around 5000mm, or 197in, a year) of this region has given rise to tea-growing and the production of tropical crops such as watermelons, bananas and sugarcane.

The Whitsunday Islands

Above Located off the central Queensland coast and well within the tropics, the beautiful Whitsunday Group of islands was first recorded by Captain James Cook on his voyage up the continent's east coast in 1770. Cook noted that the islands were 'green and pleasant', which was a fair if not exactly enthusiastic description. From the waterfront town of Airlie Beach this evening sky over the Whitsunday Passage looking towards the islands reveals high peaks and their mainland-like nature. Unlike the true Great Barrier Reef coral cays such as low-lying Heron Island to the south, these are 'continental' islands. This means that the islands are still connected to the mainland. The peaks, which once formed a coastal mountain chain, were separated by flooding. This occurred during the post-Ice Age period many thousands of years ago when sea levels were raised and the tips of the mountain range became the group of islands now known as the Whitsunday Islands. A reminder of this is found in the islands' densely forested vegetation which is very similar to that of the coast. There are fringing reefs in these waters that can be explored, and a flotilla of boats takes visitors from the busy little port of Shute Harbour each day to the islands or on sightseeing, diving, snorkelling or fishing trips to the Great Barrier Reef.

Right The Whitsunday region's warm climate, extraordinarily white beaches and brilliant blue and green waters have made this a very well-patronised holiday destination. Many of the islands contain resorts, ranging from the exclusive and expensive at Hayman Island to a 'Club Med' resort and the more family-orientated establishments on South Molle and Brampton. Others are national park islands, such as magnificent Whitsunday Island (right). These islands are totally uninhabited and attract a more low-key style of visitor who prefers to camp and appreciate the natural environment.

Despite the handful of holiday resorts, most of the 100 or so islands have changed little since Captain James Cook's day and are included in both the Whitsunday Islands National Park and the Great Barrier Reef Marine Park. The islands' dense grasslands, eucalypt forests, rainforests and pandanus groves are home to relatively few mammals and reptiles, but bird species, including ospreys and sea eagles, are abundant. The sheltered waters make the Whitsundays, which extend for around 160km (100 miles), a magnet for sailors; many people come here to hire yachts and cruisers and spend a 'get-away-from-it-all' holiday cruising peacefully from island to island to bay to inlet.

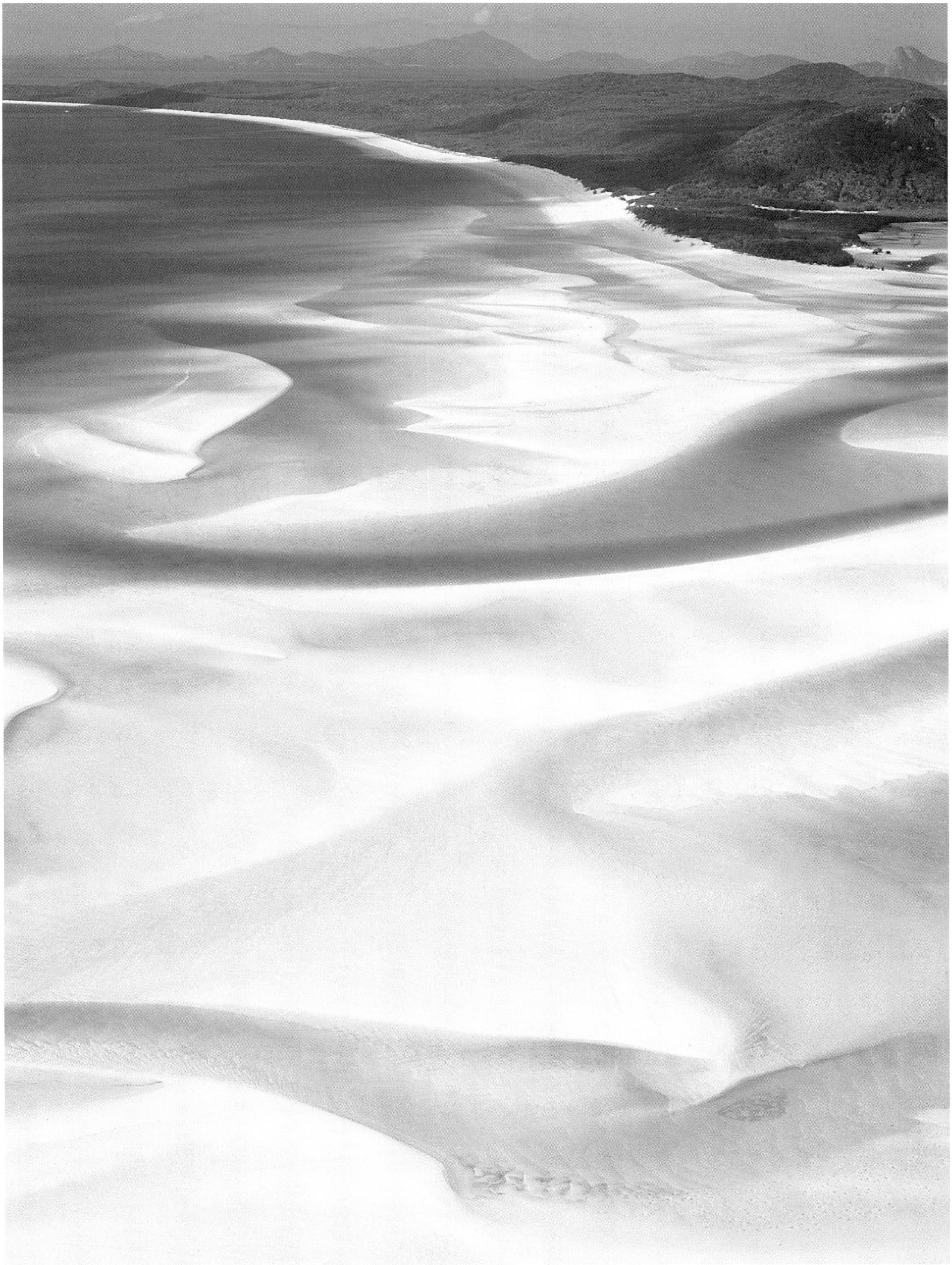

The EAST

MOUNTAINS TO SEA: A FERTILE LANDSCAPE

Despite images of Australia as a land of rugged, sparsely populated outback, it is actually one of the world's most urbanised societies. Around 88 per cent of the population lives in towns and cities – of which a large proportion is concentrated in the east and south. Australia's largest city, Sydney, is located in the east, as are Brisbane, Queensland's major city, and Canberra, the national capital. But this region, backed by the Great Dividing Range that runs for over 2500km (1554 miles), has a relatively unspoilt coastline that contains some of the country's most beautiful natural surprises.

The east coast was the birthplace for the white colonisation of Australia. The region was first charted by Captain James Cook in 1770 and then settled, at Sydney Cove, by the thousand or so convicts and soldiers of the First Fleet that arrived from England in January 1788. Although instructed to form a colony at Botany Bay, the fleet's commander sensibly probed the coastline and came upon Port Jackson (Sydney Harbour) to the north, which was a far more suitable site. The colony, initially concentrated around the harbour and today's precincts of Circular Quay, The Rocks and Royal Botanic Gardens, soon made its first timid steps towards exploring the continent.

The region of Parramatta, 22km (14 miles) from Sydney, was established a few months after the First Fleet's arrival, and the upper Hawkesbury River district around Richmond and Windsor followed soon after. Over the following decades, as thousands of convicts arrived in New South Wales, other penal colonies were established in Tasmania in 1803, at Port Macquarie north of Sydney in 1821, and at Brisbane in 1825. Norfolk Island, 1600km (994 miles) out in the Pacific Ocean, was a prison site until the 1850s but Lord Howe Island, which is closer to the coast, was spared this fate. With its World Heritage status, tiny Lord Howe is a Pacific island paradise which contrasts volcanic peaks with pristine beaches, interesting coral reefs and exceptional birdlife.

Exploration continued further into the interior of the continent when a route through the seemingly impenetrable Blue Mountains, part of the Great Dividing Range, was eventually discovered in 1813. Even today it is not really difficult to see why this area formed such a barrier to expansion. Much of the Blue Mountains region is still a wilderness of steep escarpments, caves, heavily forested valleys, rivers and rocky outcrops. Although it is not very high, and a deeply eroded sandstone plateau rather than actual mountains, this national park region is still very impressive. Beyond here, the plains settlements of Bathurst, Orange, Dubbo, Wellington and Mudgee were established as agricultural centres – a role they still fulfil today. This region later flourished with the discovery of gold in 1851, an event that boosted the colony's population quite dramatically.

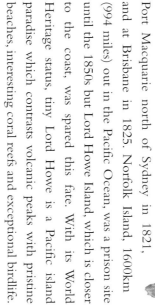

Left Despite many attempts to find a way over or around the Blue Mountains to the west of Sydney, it presented an impassable barrier to the early explorers. It was not until 1813 that a path was finally carved across these rugged and heavily forested sandstone uplands, leading to the opening up of fertile farming land west of the Great Dividing Range, and much needed expansion for the early colony.

Previous pages Australia's eastern region presents a variety of terrain – from the subtropical sugarcane-growing area of Bundaberg in Queensland to the New South Wales Snowy Mountains that are snow-covered in winter. There are also lush rainforests, surf-pounded beaches, and large tracts of fertile agricultural land, such as this wheat and cotton area around Parkes and Dubbo in mid-west New South Wales.

Eastern Australia's south coast was explored as early as 1797, and this region of rocky headlands, sandy bays, inlets and lakes offers enormously varied scenery. The coast encompasses Sydney's Royal National Park, the industrial port city of Wollongong (population 235 000), and the resort and fishing towns of Ulladulla, Batemans Bay, Bermagui, Tathra, Merimbula and Eden. The latter was established as a whaling station in the 1820s, but its industries are now timber and fishing – oysters, tuna, abalone and snapper are all caught off the coast. Eden's Ben Boyd National Park is a fragile environment of shale and sandstone with coastal heath, eucalypt woodland and the rare ground parrot, which is a vulnerable species and much is being done to preserve it. Other important sites on the south coast are Jervis Bay, with its extraordinarily white sand and clear waters, and Murramarang National Park – an environment of coastline, rainforest and eucalypts that is home to kangaroos and wallabies. The coast's hinterland is a rich dairy farming and timber region, interspersed with rugged highlands such as the limestone Deua National Park.

Further west, the Great Dividing Range reaches its zenith in Kosciusko National Park. This reserve encompasses the country's highest point (Mount Kosciusko at 2228m, or 7310ft), as well as ski resorts and stunning alpine landscapes that include the headwaters of the Murray and Murrumbidgee rivers. Once the snow has melted, these granite hills are covered with wildflowers and snow gums. It is also the habitat for many birds and animals, among them possums, wombats and grey kangaroos. This region was the scene of one of the world's most ambitious engineering projects – the 1940s to 1970s Snowy Mountains Hydro-Electric Scheme that provides power and irrigation to a large part of southern Australia through its dams and reservoirs such as Lake Eucumbene.

Well beyond the Snowy Mountains, the flat irrigated western plains form a major agricultural belt – the towns of Wagga Wagga, Griffith and Leeton service the sheep, wine, wheat, vegetable, rice and citrus fruit industries. The Murray River, which marks most of the New South Wales–Victoria border, creates a similarly fertile environment, with riverside settlements such as Albury forming important pastoral centres, particularly for the sheep and wool industries.

Bordering Kosciusko National Park, the Australian Capital Territory contains the national capital of Australia, Canberra. Created on New South Wales farming land in the early 1900s, the Territory and capital were the result of a long rivalry

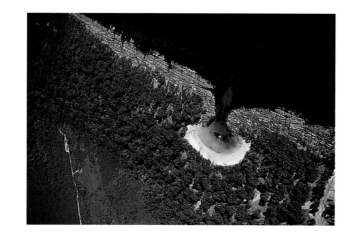

between Sydney and Melbourne for the honour of being the nation's premier city. Canberra is a planned, modern environment, but the Australian Capital Territory also encompasses natural areas such as subalpine Namadgi National Park, the Brindabella Range (once an Aboriginal food-gathering and ceremonial area) and Tidbinbilla Nature Reserve.

The Great Dividing Range continues west and north from the Snowy Mountains, creating spectacular upland areas in the inaccessible Budawang and Morton national parks, before forming the more gentle Southern Highlands. This area of picturesque towns and farming land was settled early in Australia's history, with the town of Berrima dating back to 1830. The nearby city of Goulburn also has a long agricultural tradition. It was established in 1833 when the area proved to be ideal for wheat, wool and cattle.

Sydney's north is fringed by many sandy beaches that extend to the inlet of Broken Bay. Bordered by the Ku-ring-gai Chase National Park, with its rock carvings and other evidence of Aboriginal occupation, this bay is also the outlet for the Hawkesbury River that winds its way seawards from the Blue Mountains region. Other inlets, such as Lake Macquarie (Australia's largest saltwater lake), fringe the coast between here and the major port city of Newcastle to the north. Inland, the fertile Hunter Valley nurtures a contrasting bounty – from the early 1800s both coal and wine have been extensively yielded. It remains a mystery as to who planted the valley's first vine crop, but wine from this region has gained a huge international reputation – not the least because the vineyards have become a prime tourist attraction through tastings and cellar-door sales.

From here to the Queensland border the Pacific Ocean coast is dotted with holiday towns and magnificent natural features. Myall Lakes National Park is an unusual blend of bushland, rainforest, lakes, dunes and beaches, with wildlife in the form of kangaroos, echidnas, pelicans and black swans. Beyond the lakes, the coastline includes beaches, national parks and small resort towns such as Port Macquarie, while the hinterland's rich dairy and timber areas are located around the towns of Taree, Wingham and Gloucester. The city of Coffs Harbour marks the start of a subtropical zone that attracts many holiday-makers and also supports fruit and vegetable growing. Further north, Grafton is the centre of a sugarcane and dairy farming area and Byron Bay, with its superb beaches and subtropical hinterland, is a popular resort with a majestic lighthouse set upon the cape, Australia's easternmost point.

Inland, the Great Dividing Range rises to elevated areas such as the glorious Barrington Tops, part of the World Heritage-listed East Coast Temperate and Subtropical Rainforest Parks. Encompassing 16 separate reserves, and including the superb Dorrigo National Park, this area of temperate and subtropical forests, rivers, escarpments and waterfalls protects a once heavily logged region. Mount Warning, the core of what was originally a vast volcano, casts a dramatic figure on this inland environment. Between these uplands and the flat western plains lie some of the most important agricultural towns in New South Wales – Tamworth, Armidale, Glen Innes, Inverell and Tenterfield.

A very different scene emerges just beyond the Queensland border. Once a quiet strip of surf and sandy beaches, the Gold Coast is now a major modern tourist centre with high-rise buildings, theme parks and many glitzy attractions. Inland from the coast, in contrast, there are natural scenic areas such as Lamington National Park, with its subtropical rainforest,

rugged heights and varied wildlife, including bandicoots, lyrebirds and goannas. Further west, the rich farming lands of the Granite Belt and Darling Downs around Stanthorpe, Warwick and Toowoomba grow a wide variety of produce, including cereals, vegetables, dairy products, wool and wine.

From its convict origins in the early 1800s, the subtropical city of Brisbane has grown into a modern metropolis with a population of some 1.3 million people. Situated on the Brisbane River, with the large expanse of Moreton Bay providing a recreation area, Brisbane is one of the nation's most relaxed cities. Moreton Bay, once a rich source of fish and shellfish for large Aboriginal communities, features several islands, including the national park of Moreton Island, which has dunes, heathland, forest and lakes.

Inland, the Glasshouse Mountains, remnants of ancient lava flows, rise dramatically from the plains and herald the start of the Sunshine Coast. Encompassing the attractive resorts of Caloundra, Mooloolaba, Maroochydore and Noosa Heads, this coastline is far more low-key than the glossy Gold Coast. In addition to its headlands and sandy beaches, this region contains the waterways of the Noosa River system and the forests and grasslands of Noosa National Park. Part of the great sand belt that includes Moreton Island and Fraser Island to the north, Cooloola National Park is a coastal wilderness of dunes, forest, heathland, swamps and waterways. The towering multi-coloured sand cliffs of Rainbow Beach are a magnificent backdrop to the township – perhaps 40 000 years old, these cliffs stretch for 30km (19 miles) and contain over 70 shades of sand. Inland, the hills and waterfalls of the Blackall Range provide a striking contrast to this coastal playground.

Opposite One of the gems of the New South Wales south coast, Jervis Bay is a pristine environment of blue waters and dazzling sand (rumoured to be the world's whitest), such as here at Honeymoon Bay.

Above The 'mighty' Murray River forms the border between New South Wales and Victoria and from 1850 onwards provided access to inland towns. Paddle-steamers became the vital link between ports, and today they are a wonderful way to explore Australia's principal river.

Right In addition to its excellent resort facilities, the Sunshine Coast features the magnificent Noosa National Park. This 432ha (1067 acres) area of coastline, grassland, forest and heathland includes rocky headlands and quiet pandanus-fringed beaches, such as this one at Tea Tree Bay.

The Great Barrier Reef, in the form of the reef islands of Lady Elliot and Lady Musgrave, reaches its southernmost extremity off the port of Gladstone: these islands are true coral cays and provide a haven for a myriad seabirds and turtles. Northwards of here, the Tropic of Capricorn 'crosses' the coast near Rockhampton and the continent's tropics begin.

The centrepiece of Australia's east coast is Sydney. The nation's birthplace has flourished since its humble beginnings in 1788 and become a world-class city of 4 million people. Blessed with its glittering harbour, long coastline dotted with beautiful beaches and the nearby semiwilderness areas of the Blue Mountains, Ku-ring-gai Chase and Royal national parks, Sydney is indeed fortunate in its location – an accident of history, perhaps, but a happy one.

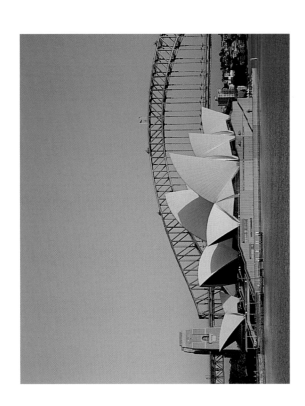

Nearby Fraser Island, the world's largest sand island (123km, or 76 miles, long) and one of Australia's 11 World Heritage sites, features the coloured 'teewah' cliffs – ancient sand deposits that have been stained by minerals. This is one of the few places where extensive rainforests grow on pure sand and the island's vegetation is dense – rainforest, ferns and wildflowers all flourish here, as do animals such as dingoes, brumbies (wild horses), possums, wallabies, echidnas and around 240 bird species. Fraser Island also contains over 40 freshwater lakes as well as several large sand blows – dunes that move with the prevailing wind. Migrating humpback whales pass through the Great Sandy Strait, between Fraser Island and Hervey Bay on the mainland, from August to October each year and provide this very special region with another wildlife highlight.

On the mainland, the fertile soils around Maryborough have led to extensive sugarcane growing – the main focus, too, for nearby Bundaberg. The city of Bundaberg is also famous for its rum and for the turtle nesting site at Mon Repos beach. Loggerhead, leatherback and rare flatback turtles nest here, and the area was once a feasting site for Aboriginal people.

Above left Sydney Opera House occupies a prominent harbourside position north of the city centre. It took 14 years to complete and was opened in 1973 by Queen Elizabeth II. It has five performance spaces and also hosts ballet, concerts, and theatrical performances.

Above The massive Sydney Harbour Bridge represented a remarkable feat of engineering when it was completed in 1932. The bridge's often congested eight traffic lanes have been supplemented by the Sydney Harbour Tunnel, which opened in the early 1990s.

Left Brisbane, the capital city of Queensland, is the nation's third-largest city after Sydney and Melbourne. Despite a 1980s building boom and increasing sophistication, this once sleepy subtropical metropolis is still a very relaxed place. Founded as a penal colony, the city is located on the Brisbane River.

Opposite Parliament House, which was completed at a cost of over A$1000 million for Australia's 1988 bicentenary, dominates Canberra from its prominent site on Capital Hill. This futuristic granite, glass and steel building is the heartland of Australian federal politics.

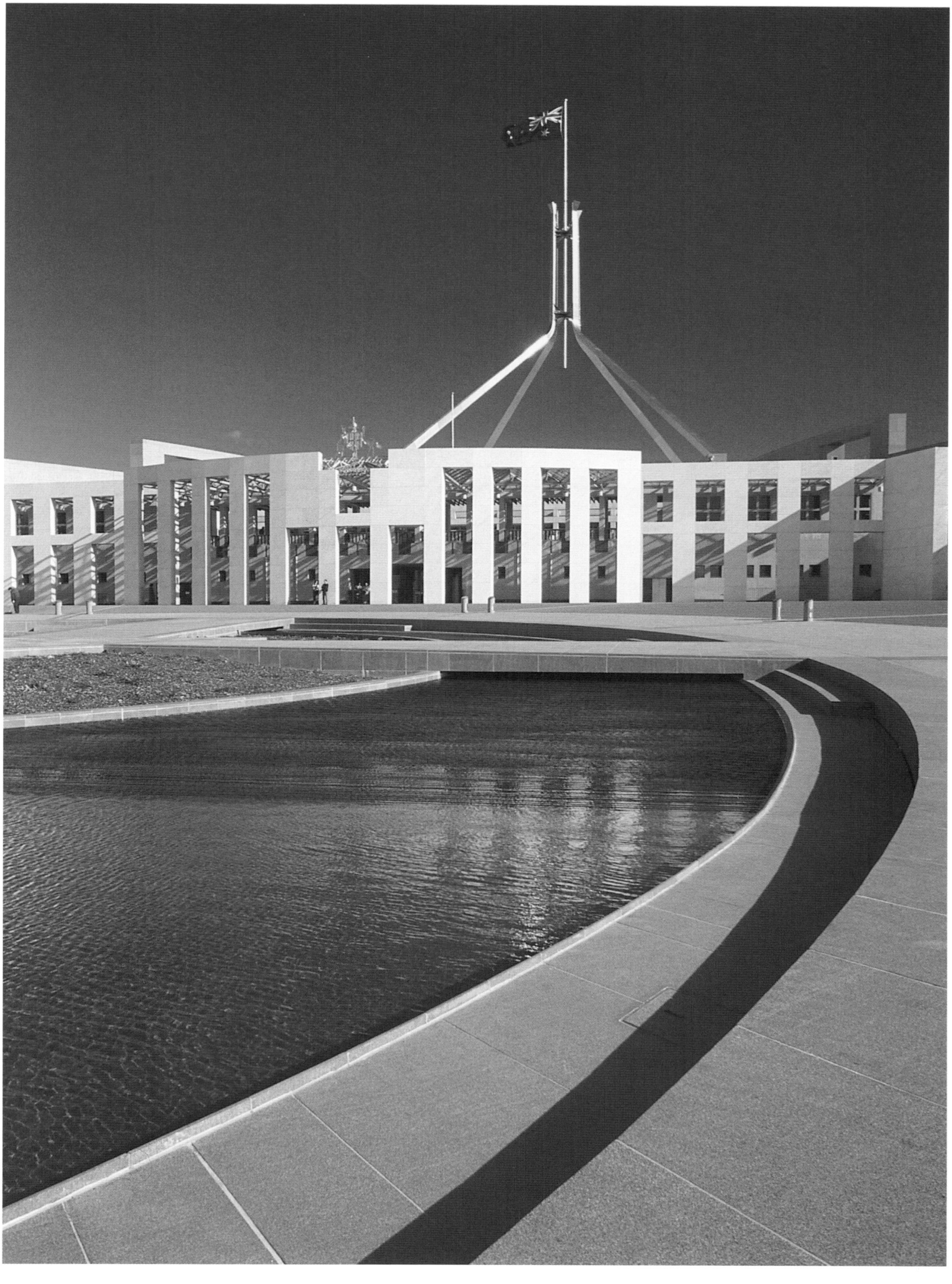

Lady Elliot and Lady Musgrave islands

Opposite The Great Barrier Reef, which runs parallel to the Queensland coast for approximately 2300km (1429 miles) from north of Cape York to south of the port of Gladstone, reaches its southern limit in the vicinity of Lady Elliot Island. In contrast with many of Queensland's so-called Barrier Reef islands, Lady Elliot is located right on the reef and is a true coral cay, with the offshore waters protected as part of the vast Great Barrier Reef Marine Park. In addition to the wonderful variety of coral and brightly coloured fish, the island is a nesting site for turtles from November until March, and whales also pass by here during the July to October migration period. Seabirds abound too, and the summer nesting season is a very busy time as the rookeries then become packed with noisy birdlife.

Named after the ship of the same name which passed by the island on its way to Sydney in 1816, Lady Elliot Island has a small, low-key holiday resort which attracts divers as well as those in search of a natural experience. The island features its own airstrip which receives regular flights from Bundaberg, but tourist numbers are strictly limited to preserve this very special environment. The diving and snorkelling here are superb and the island's 'on top of the reef' location makes it particularly appealing to underwater enthusiasts.

Above Lady Musgrave Island is another coral cay, but unlike its neighbour this is a national park with no resort facilities. Campers are welcome but numbers are restricted, all water and supplies must be shipped from the mainland, and the lack of facilities deters all but the most ardent nature lovers. Like Lady Elliot, this sandy cay is very low-lying and covered predominantly with pandanus palms, casuarinas and grasses: there is no soil as such and the vegetation grows from a bed of compost that is made up of leaves and bird droppings. Lady Musgrave is a small island – just 14ha (35 acres) – but surrounded by a clear blue lagoon and almost 5km (3 miles) of reef. The birdlife here is prolific with more than 50 species such as wedge-tailed shearwaters, reef herons and white-capped noddy terns visiting the island. The isle is a nesting site for turtles, including the green and loggerhead varieties, which lay their eggs here from October onwards. Offshore, the lagoon and reef contain hundreds of fish species, many of which are impossibly brightly coloured, as well as a variety of both hard and soft corals.

Fraser Island

Above At 123km (76 miles) long and an average of 14km (9 miles) wide, Fraser Island, off the southern Queensland coast, is one of Australia's biggest islands. Originally called Great Sandy Island by James Cook, it is also the world's largest sand island and so unique that it was included on the World Heritage register in 1992. Named after sea captain James Fraser and his wife Eliza, who were shipwrecked here in 1836, the island has been the graveyard for many ships. The wreck of the old luxury liner Maheno, which met its end in 1935, still lies on the east coast and now forms a popular tourist attraction – although its deteriorating state makes a close inspection potentially dangerous.

Below Formed over millions of years by silica and other deposits washed down from the Great Dividing Range, Fraser Island is composed almost entirely of various types, consistencies and colours of sand. The most fascinating of these is the ancient 'teewah' (meaning coloured) variety. Found along the eastern coast and often forming cliffs, the sands come in subtly tinged shades of cream, beige, ochre and pink, as well as reddish-brown, as revealed by these curious formations. The colours have been created by mineral staining over a long period of time. The island's other curious formations are sand blows – giant dunes that shift with the winds, threatening to overtake all in their path.

Above Although large parts of the island are flat, Fraser's most surprising features are its sand cliffs, its dense vegetation and over 40 freshwater lakes. Located mostly in the south, these include Lake Boomanjin, one of the island's unusual above-sea-level lakes that are 'perched' in the dunes.

Above Rainforest, such as this at the old Central Station logging site, is far from what one would expect on a sand island. Unfortunately, timber was logged on Fraser Island for a century from the 1860s and, more recently, sand mining caused an outcry until it was halted in 1976.

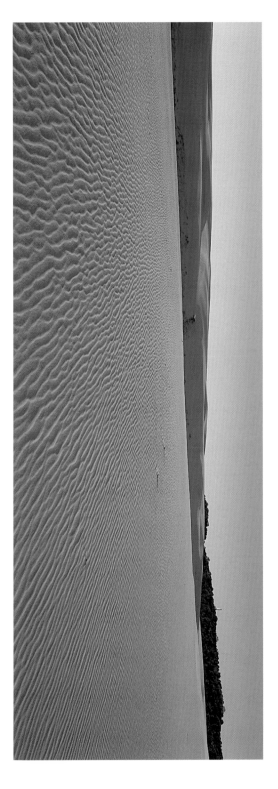

Above At Fraser Island's northern tip the Sandy Cape Lighthouse, erected in 1870 to warn shipping of the area's dangers, rises out of the rippled sand. There are no roads on the island, and a four-wheel-drive vehicle is necessary to get around in this extraordinary sandy environment.

Left In addition to its World Heritage listing, a large part of Fraser Island is protected by the Great Sandy National Park with its forest, lakes, coloured sand cliffs and coastline. This deserted eastern beach, near the wreck of the Maheno, reveals why the island is a popular destination for naturalists, birdwatchers and nature lovers.

Above A glorious sunset illuminates Lake Boomanjin as gold-tinged clouds are reflected in its waters. This large lake, in Fraser Island's south, 'perches' incredibly above sea level among the dunes and rests on an ancient bed of peat. This and the island's other lakes are surrounded by vegetation that thrives in a watery environment. The island is mostly undeveloped, with just a couple of small villages on the east coast and an upmarket 'eco-resort' in the west. Bordering the Great Sandy Strait and facing the mainland south of Hervey Bay, the coast is popular for watching humpback whales on their annual migration. There are also over 200 bird species here, including kingfishers, peregrine falcons and the stork-like jabiru. The island is a paradise for ornithologists.

Below Fraser Island is home to considerable numbers of marsupials and other animals. Wallabies, possums and echidnas thrive here, as do brumbies — wild horses descended from those brought over from the mainland in the 19th century. Dingoes are also found on Fraser Island, and in their isolation they have become the purest breed of their species remaining in eastern Australia. Although sometimes called the native dog, the dingo was a latecomer to the continent, with its arrival just 6000 years ago. Dingoes are related to domestic dogs and will breed with them, but they do not bark and they breed only once a year.

Sugarcane farming near Bundaberg

Above The Bundaberg region of central Queensland has long been at the heart of a prolific sugarcane-growing industry. The first cane crops were grown here back in 1869 – a result of the region's rich basaltic soils and the inspiration of local pioneers. By the 1880s the sugarcane industry had flourished to such an extent that a shortage of labour threatened to slow its development. The highly unethical solution was to import labourers from the South Sea Islands – known as Kanakas, these men were often press-ganged into leaving their homes, and treated very badly on arrival in Queensland. Paid a mere pittance, the unfortunate 'migrants' were forced to labour at the hard physical work of clearing, planting and cutting by hand, in rough conditions and under the fierce subtropical sun.

At the end of the 1880s, Bundaberg boasted around 40 sugar mills and rum had by this time become an important by-product. The city is famous for its Bundaberg Rum, known throughout Australia as 'Bundy', and the nation's most popular home-grown spirit. These flat cane fields reveal the area's dark, rich soil and the low growth of new sugarcane, but fully mature cane becomes incredibly dense and can reach a height of up to 4m (13ft).

Right This may look like an out of control bushfire, or a scene of devastation, but man-made fires are a common seasonal sight around Bundaberg and in Queensland's more northerly sugarcane-growing regions. The cane, a giant tropical grass, takes 12–16 months to mature: it is harvested between July and November, and 'firing' is a traditional pre-harvesting procedure. Although it is now increasingly common for cane to be harvested green rather than burnt, firing removes weeds, leaves and other debris which impede the crop's processing. Sugarcane is usually burnt in the late afternoon and evening – it burns rapidly and high-shooting flames create a spectacular sight to rival the sunsets in the countryside around Bundaberg.

Harvesting cane was once a backbreaking and laborious procedure done by hand but nowadays it is harvested by machine, cut into short pieces and then transported to the mills by special cane trains. These trains and their tracks crisscross the countryside wherever the crop is grown. The Bundaberg region, with around 1400 sugarcane farms and four mills, produces about a fifth of all Australia's sugar, which is exported in vast quantities in its raw state to countries such as the USA, China, Japan and New Zealand.

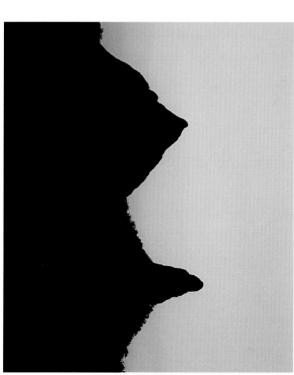

The Glasshouse Mountains

Left *Not far from the Bruce Highway which runs between Brisbane and the Sunshine Coast, the strangely shaped Glasshouse Mountains loom out of the otherwise rather flat landscape. So named by James Cook in 1770 because they reminded him of the glass furnaces of his native Yorkshire, the peaks are actually volcanic plugs – remnants of solidified lava flows that were part of a vast but long extinct volcano. Four national parks encompass some of the 11 peaks, as well as the heath, rainforest and eucalypt forest that surround them. The area, which is home to wildlife such as koalas, echidnas and wallabies, is particularly popular with bushwalkers as well as rock climbers. Looking towards the coast from this hinterland farm, the mountains are a very distinctive feature of the southern Queensland landscape.*

Above *Mount Beerwah (left) at 556m (1824ft) high and Mount Coonowrin (an Aboriginal word meaning 'crookneck') at 375m (1230ft) are the two highest peaks of the Glasshouse Mountains, which are believed to have been formed approximately 20 million years ago. An Aboriginal legend refers to these peaks (near Mount Tibrogargan) and several others as a family of father, mother, elder son and younger children. Seen in silhouette at sunset, the distinctive peaks do indeed resemble strange figures from another, more mystical, world.*

Dalby

Following pages *The area known as the Darling Downs, in the far south-east of Queensland, is an extremely fertile agricultural region that produces much of the state's essential foodstuffs as well as other important commodities such as wool. Initially developed by cattle farmers in the 1840s, the black soil plains of the downs now yield vast amounts of wheat, maize, cotton and other crops, and also support cattle, sheep, pigs and poultry. These silos near the town of Dalby store large quantities of grain which end up in the area's many flour mills.*

Lamington National Park

Above Inland from Queensland's Gold Coast, the green expanse of Lamington National Park provides a contrast to the high-rise buildings and crowds of tourists less than 50km (31 miles) away. This park preserves the little that remains of south-east Queensland's pristine subtropical rainforest, and is a moist upland environment of densely wooded hills and mountains, cliffs and waterfalls. Some of Lamington's most intriguing plants are the xanthorrhoeas, or grasstrees. These archaic trees, found only in Australia, consist of solid dark trunks, long narrow leaves, and a thin extended spike which is covered with tiny flowers. Xanthorrhoeas have grown on the continent for as long as 100 million years and are supreme survivors, with the ability to resist the most severe conditions created by drought, flood and fire.

Right Panoramic views are a highlight of Lamington, which covers terrain from the McPherson Range to the valleys far below. This variation in altitude means that the park's flora ranges from dense rainforest and many orchid species in its lower reaches through to flame trees and, on the cool plateau, stands of ancient Antarctic beech trees. The park is popular with walkers, climbers and nature lovers, but also provides the perfect environment for a wide variety of bird and animal life. Rainbow lorikeets, king parrots and crimson rosellas abound here, as do small, curiously named marsupials such as possums, potoroos, bandicoots and pademelons.

The North Coast of New South Wales

Opposite North of the resort of Tweed Heads, New South Wales merges almost imperceptibly into Queensland. This coastline contains long stretches of marvellous beaches that draw holidaymakers from both states. Boating, fishing and surfing are popular around Tweed Heads, but a stark contrast lies further north. Queensland's glossy Gold Coast, based around the town of Surfers Paradise, is home to high-rise hotels, holiday flats, theme parks, a casino and shopping arcades. At dusk the coast's lights can be seen in the distance from this Tweed Heads beach.

Above The most northerly town in New South Wales, Tweed Heads is at the mouth of the Tweed River which winds its way from the Great Dividing Range. The lighthouse stands appropriately on Point Danger – a dire warning to ships, and named by Captain Cook after the near wrecking of the Endeavour on the offshore reefs in 1770.

Below From Cape Byron, Australia's most easterly point, the often deserted beaches stretch north to the Queensland border, 80km (50 miles) away. This is one of the east coast's favourite holiday areas, offering a lush subtropical hinterland and picturesque towns and villages in addition to superb beaches and a host of water sports. Named by James Cook, the cape commemorates not the legendary poet but rather his seafaring grandfather – the navigator Captain John Byron.

Following pages Viewed from Muttonbird Island, Coffs Harbour is a yachting haven as well as a mecca for surf, sun and sand lovers. This settlement is the New South Wales north coast's premier beach and tourist resort, and also the home of a large fishing fleet. Further inland, the forested hills of the Great Dividing Range slope down to fertile farming land, where subtropical fruits such as bananas are cultivated.

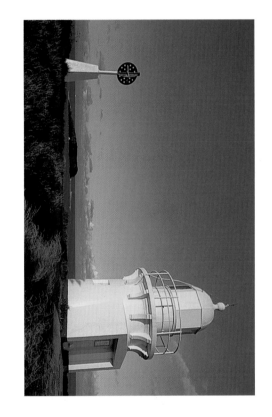

Glen Innes

Above The granite region around the agricultural and mining town of Glen Innes, in the north of New South Wales, has given rise to some curiously shaped rock formations. The strange Balancing Rock, off the highway to the south of town, is perhaps the most famous. It has been estimated that this large boulder balances on a mere 30cm (12in) contact point. The local granite has been used extensively in the region for building purposes, including the town's impressive 1870s courthouse.

Dorrigo National Park

Right Richly deserving its World Heritage status, Dorrigo National Park is a pristine environment of orchids, ferns, rainforest and waterfalls which experiences particularly high rainfall. The park is based around the dramatic Dorrigo escarpment which falls steeply to the surrounding lowland. This reserve of lush greenery, inland from the seaside resort of Coffs Harbour, supports over 120 bird species, including brush turkeys and spectacular lyrebirds, and mammals such as wallabies and possums.

Myall Lakes National Park

Left Just 90km (56 miles) from Newcastle lies one of the state's most attractive reserves. The Myall Lakes National Park, encompassing a stretch of coastal lakes, often deserted beaches and offshore islands, is a superb environment that attracts thousands of visitors each year. The park's waterways form one of the largest coastal lake systems in New South Wales, and are ideal for waterbirds such as sea eagles, cranes, black swans and ducks. There are endless possibilities for recreation, including bushwalking, boating, canoeing, fishing, sailboarding, and scuba diving off the unspoilt coastline separated from the lakes by a chain of sand dunes. The rich vegetation features tall eucalypts, wattles, rainforest trees, and waterside paperbarks and casuarinas like these pictured; wildlife in the park includes wallabies, grey kangaroos, goannas and echidnas.

Barrington Tops National Park

Below North-west of Myall Lakes, Barrington Tops National Park forms part of the World Heritage-listed East Coast Temperate and Sub-tropical Rainforest Parks. Made up of 16 areas, this 'park' preserves a region of rainforest types, including subtropical, dry, warm temperate and cool temperate, which have been spared from the clearing and logging that has destroyed so much of New South Wales' forest land.

Lying high on the Hunter Valley's northern escarpment, Barrington Tops encompasses a range of altitudes and corresponding vegetation. There are swamps and subtropical rainforests, uplands with Antarctic beech trees, and even snow in winter. This park also provides a habitat for kangaroos, wallabies, possums, reptiles and a host of birdlife.

Sydney

Previous pages At any time of the day Sydney Harbour dazzles, but at sunset it is truly spectacular. It's hard to imagine that it was only an accident of history that brought the First Fleeters north from Botany Bay to this beautiful expanse of water in Port Jackson. The star attraction, of course, is Sydney Harbour Bridge which for many years provided the only link at this section of the harbour between north and south. The silhouette of the bridge and the famous Opera House are instantly recognisable under this fiery glow.

Left The most famous beach in Sydney would have to be Bondi. Most tourists who arrive in Sydney seem to have this ocean beach, situated only 8km (5 miles) from the city centre, on their list of places to visit. In summer the sands are packed with beach revellers.

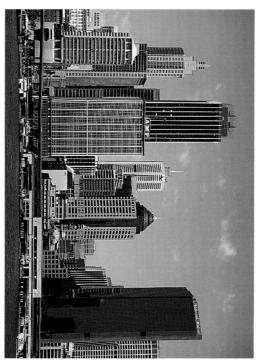

Above Sydney's city skyline has changed enormously over the last 200 years. Once these shores were covered in dense forests of gum trees, but with the march of time it is now the buildings that grow taller and fight for space. Just to the right of the city centre and dwarfed by the modern buildings is the clock tower of Customs House, built in 1888. Passing the front of the city, the Cahill Expressway leads onto the bridge. Circular Quay in the foreground is the main terminus for ferries.

Left Ferries provide a wonderful way to see the harbour, and a glorious start and finish to the working day. Many city workers can opt to travel to their offices by this means as ferries quickly travel to and from Circular Quay to the eastern suburbs, the north shore, Manly and the inner west. There is even a ferry that travels under the bridge past Goat Island and down the Parramatta River to the western suburbs. A more leisurely pace can also be enjoyed with tour operators providing a variety of cruises that explore the bays and coves of Sydney Harbour.

Below On 26 January each year the harbour bustles as Australians celebrate Australia Day. This is the anniversary of the arrival in Sydney Cove of the first Europeans. The annual Ferry Race provides colour as the ferries race to see who can be the first under the bridge. Anybody who has a boat joins in the festivities and spectators with picnic hampers crowd the foreshores to watch. Fireworks often complete the day, showering colour over the city skyline, bridge and Opera House.

Blue Mountains National Park

Above One of the highlights of the Blue Mountains National Park, less than 100km (62 miles) west of Sydney, is the famous Three Sisters rock formation. This view, from the lookout at Echo Point in the town of Katoomba, looks beyond the 'Sisters' and across the forested Jamison Valley to the rugged ridges at the park's southern edge. Although the 'mountains' are relatively low in elevation – the highest point is only 1065m (3494ft) above sea level – and comprise an eroded plateau rather than a series of peaks, the scenery is undeniably dramatic.

The sandstone that makes up Three Sisters is the national park's best known geological feature, and the pillars are also the subject of Aboriginal myth – according to the legend, the 'Sisters' were turned to stone to save them from falling into the hands of a monster. Aboriginal people lived in this upland region for at least 14 000 years, and evidence of their occupation remains today in the form of axe grinding grooves, rock engravings and drawings.

Opposite The rugged Blue Mountains, so called because the air in the region often appears to be a bluish colour (a phenomenon caused by the evaporation of eucalyptus oil from the gum tree forests), formed a barrier to exploration for the first 25 years of the colony's life. This section of the Great Dividing Range is distinguished by escarpments, forested valleys and spectacular rock features like this at Hanging Rock, which frustrated many early explorers in their search for a route over the mountains.

The Blue Mountains National Park encompasses over 200 000ha (494 200 acres) of wild terrain. South of the Great Western Highway, which winds its way along a ridge and follows the route that was tracked across the mountains in 1813, the escarpment falls away into the Jamison Valley. To the north, the Grose Valley forms another break in the plateau. This wilderness is popular with bushwalkers, and the area is home to swamp wallabies, possums, wombats and an incredible range of colourful birdlife.

Morton National Park

Above Morton National Park runs 97km (60 miles) along the rim and slopes of a high sandstone plateau in the rural and largely unspoilt Southern Highlands, west of Nowra. The Illawarra escarpment falls mostly within the boundaries of the park and creates a wild and rugged vista which rivals the Blue Mountains. There are many waterfalls, the most spectacular being the Fitzroy Falls which plunge 82m (269ft) into the fertile valley below. A number of walking tracks to the east and west of the falls offer wonderful views of the cascading water and of the surrounding bushland. In this area old-man banksia, thin-leaved stringy-bark, urn-fruited peppermint and scribbly gum trees abound, along with many species of shrubs. The park's vast variety of landforms and vegetation is home to many animals including grey kangaroos, swamp and red-necked wallabies, snakes, lizards, wedge-tailed and whistling eagles, lyrebirds, parrots, eastern bristle birds and the rare ground parrot which is a vulnerable species.

Left On the fringes of the Morton National Park is Manning Lookout which offers stunning views of the tranquil Kangaroo Valley. This region was first explored in 1818, only 30 years after the arrival of the First Fleet, by Dr Charles Throsby. He and his party paved the way for farmers to move into this haven. They were followed by prospectors looking for silver, gold, copper, tin, lead and zinc. Kangaroo Valley is one of the prettiest vales in New South Wales with a patchwork of farms within the rainforested slopes of the Illawarra escarpment. The whole valley, along with the township (which has a mediaeval-style stone suspension bridge built in 1898), has been classified by the National Trust as worth preserving – a very high distinction indeed.

A land of contrasts

Opposite The Snowy Mountains region of southern New South Wales is not only famous for its rugged upland scenery; the area contains the dams, reservoirs, tunnels and aqueducts of the Snowy Mountains Scheme – an enormous hydro-electric and irrigation project which diverts and stores the waters of the Snowy, Eucumbene and Murrumbidgee rivers. Lake Jindabyne is part of this world-famous engineering feat which took 25 years to achieve and was completed in 1974.

Above Although merely a narrow coastal strip, Murramarang National Park, north of Batemans Bay on the New South Wales south coast, protects a superb environment of shoreline and forest. The sandy beaches and rugged headlands are backed by lush forest, and eastern grey kangaroos are seen here in large numbers – even on the park's many beaches.

Right In the relatively remote far south of New South Wales, Ben Boyd National Park contains one of the state's most pristine coastal areas. Pounding surf, beautiful beaches, and fascinating geological cliff, cave and rock formations are the highlights of the park, named after Benjamin Boyd, an enterprising migrant who developed the Eden area in the 1840s.

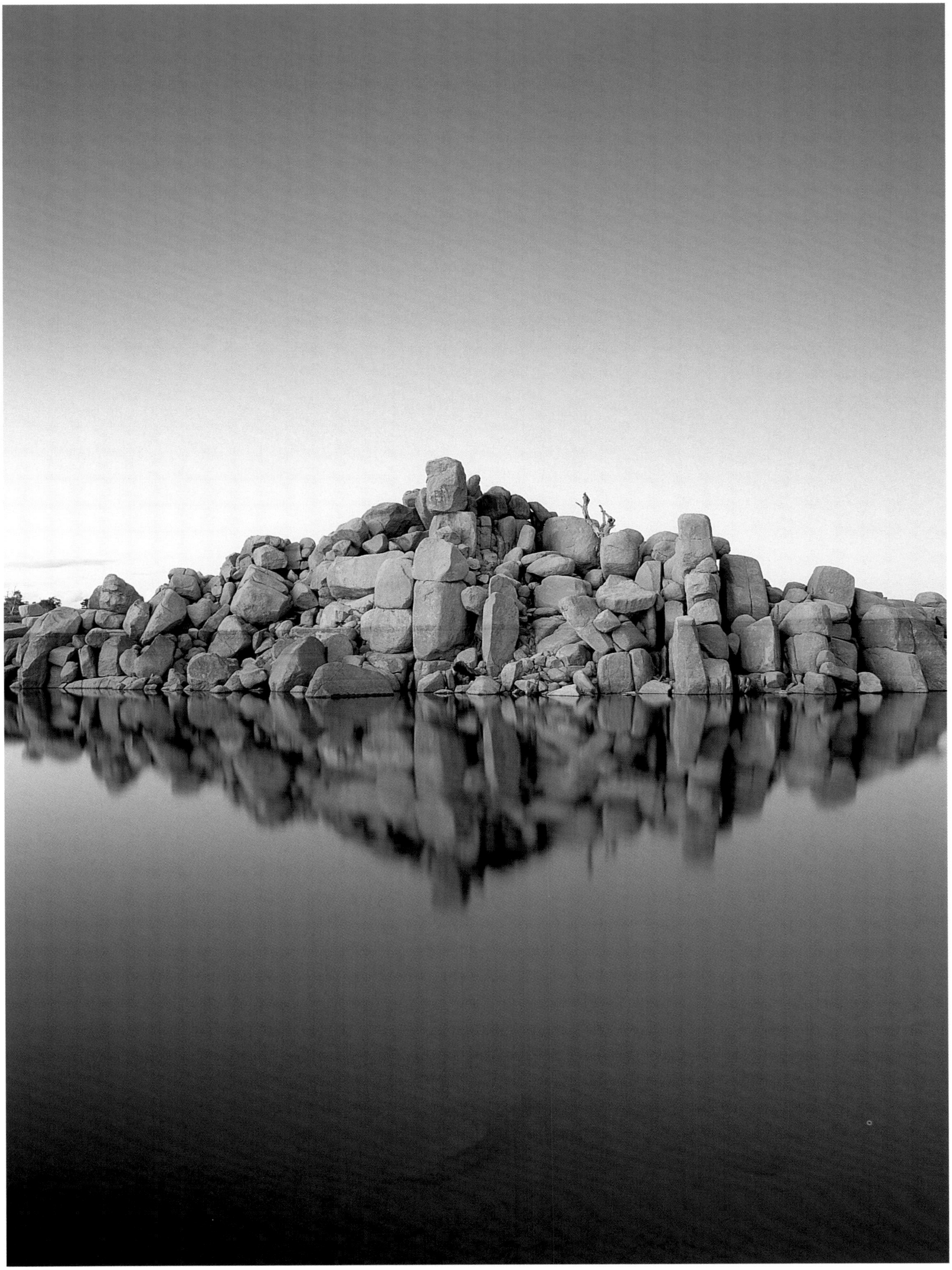

The CENTRE

RED EARTH AND BLUE SKIES: AN UNTAMED LAND

Australia's vast, arid outback, also known as the 'Red Centre', 'Dead Heart' or simply the 'Centre', takes up about 70 per cent of the continent and encompasses some of the most desolate country on earth. Including portions of Western Australia, the Northern Territory, South Australia, Queensland and New South Wales, the Centre is an incredibly harsh yet unique and starkly beautiful environment. In this region temperatures can soar as high as 55°C (131°F), yet they can also plummet to 5°C (41°F) on winter nights. Despite its mineral riches, water is the most precious commodity in this drought-prone land, and most of the isolated outback settlements are almost totally reliant on artesian bore water extracted from far beneath the earth's parched surface. Life is often very hard and uncomfortable, yet this inhospitable region supports a substantial number of both indigenous and non-Aboriginal Australians.

Much of the outback is desert – almost two-thirds of Western Australia, for example, is taken up by the red rock, sand dunes and dry salt lakes of the Great Sandy, Gibson and Great Victoria deserts. Similarly in South Australia, a large proportion of the state is taken up by the seemingly endless tracts of the dune-ribbed Simpson Desert, and the Strzelecki and Sturts Stony deserts – the latter strewn with the hard round stones known as gibbers (from an Aboriginal word, 'giba', for stone) – compose a large proportion of the state. This area contains many dry 'waterways' and also Lake Eyre, the world's largest salt pan with a catchment

area of a massive 1.3 million km² (501 800 sq miles). The region's sparse rainfall, however, means that these lakes and rivers are persistently dry, and Lake Eyre fills only a couple of times every hundred years.

The vast deserts eventually give way to still arid, sparsely inhabited areas such as 'Corner Country', a region of gibber plains and sandhills that includes remote Cameron Corner, the point where the borders of South Australia, New South Wales and Queensland meet. In western Queensland, the desert reluctantly makes way for the 'Channel Country' (so named because of its very intricate web of intermittently water-fed creeks and rivers) situated around the tiny settlement of Birdsville.

This stark aridity, however, gives the Centre an undeniable rugged beauty and contains many internationally acclaimed natural wonders. In addition to dozens of national parks, this region is the home of two of Australia's 11 UNESCO World Heritage-listed sites: Uluru–Katatjuta National Park, encompassing Uluru (Ayers Rock) and Katatjuta (the Olgas) and listed for both its natural and cultural values, and the Willandra Lakes region in the Mungo National Park of south-west New South Wales. This latter site has yielded the archaeological treasures of Lake Mungo's 30 000-year-old remains of 'Mungo Man', the fossils of extinct animals and prehistoric stone tools.

Left Uluru symbolises the stark beauty of Australia's outback. Known and revered by Aborigines since prehistoric times, it was 'discovered' by explorer Ernest Giles in 1872 and then named Ayers Rock after the Premier of South Australia. It reverted to its Aboriginal name, Uluru, when custodianship of the Uluru–Katatjuta National Park was handed back to the Yankuntjatjara and Pitjantjatjara people.

Previous pages As this desolate scene illustrates, the centre of Australia is harsh and unforgiving. It has defied most attempts to tame it, but with its seemingly limitless blue horizons, rich ochre and terracotta colours and sense of space and tranquillity the outback can be surprisingly beautiful. After rain, for example, the apparently barren terrain often springs to life with colourful wildflowers.

Left Because of its very trying nature, the rugged outback has bred and attracted many courageous and offbeat 'characters' – which may be a case of hardship leading to humour rather than despair: farmers of the region are under the constant threat of drought which can deplete their stock and livelihood; the vast distances mean the residents often lead lonely, isolated lives; and facilities taken for granted in cities are either few or non-existent. Although life is tough here, these miners, cattle and sheep farmers, and the flying doctors, School of the Air teachers, shop-keepers and others that serve the pastoral industry are essentially far more laid-back than Australia's city populations. They speak more slowly, take more time to chat, know how to enjoy their leisure time, and have the greatest respect for the unpredictable land they inhabit.

There are few true waterways in the outback, much of which experiences an average rainfall of less than 250mm (10in) a year. A notable exception is the 2800km-long (1740 miles) Darling River, running from northern New South Wales to the Murray River, which forms the border of New South Wales and Victoria and was once important for trade and communications. The now sleepy backwater of Wilcannia on the Darling River was once, too, an important centre, having been at one time Australia's third-largest inland port. The Darling River incorporates the Menindee Lakes, a group which includes the Menindee, Wetherell, Pamamaroo and Cawndilla lakes. They provide an important water-storage system embraced by Kinchega National Park, which as a result is a rich environment for waterbirds and eucalypts.

It is not surprising that this arid land appears to support very little vegetation. After heavy rains, however, the deserts come alive as long-dormant seeds bloom into colourful wildflowers, including the red and black Sturt's desert pea and many daisy species. Such unusually heavy rainfall can also cause widespread flooding as normally parched water channels struggle to contain the unfamiliar flow. Much of the desert is dotted with little more than low-growing, drought-resistant plants such as saltbush, prickly spinifex and mulga, a variety of the widespread acacia. In some areas larger trees – the pale-trunked ghost gums, mallees and river red gums (found around watercourses) – are common. A more exotic form of vegetation is offered, however, by Palm Valley in the Northern Territory's Finke Gorge National Park. The 3000 or so cabbage palms here are several hundred years old and form a lush oasis among the rugged rocks and gorges.

Although most of the interior is flat and featureless, the monotony is broken intermittently by ranges, hills, gorges and isolated rock outcrops. The most famous of these is Uluru, an important Aboriginal sacred site as well as one of Australia's major icons and tourist attractions. Located in the Northern Territory at the very heart of the continent, this 348m-high

Left Although a large percentage of the Red Centre consists of desert, the scenery in this region is actually much more varied than might be imagined. These high sand dunes in the Simpson Desert, at the very heart of the continent, form a very striking contrast to the nearby rock-strewn Sturts Stony Desert.

Opposite Australia's outback contains many vast, dry and salty lakebeds that only occasionally fill with water after very heavy rain. Lake Callabonna in South Australia is one such waterless lake, but this lake is also the site of some rather remarkable archaeological finds. The remnants of prehistoric animals, including the fossilised diprotodon, the Australian continent's largest marsupial, have been discovered here.

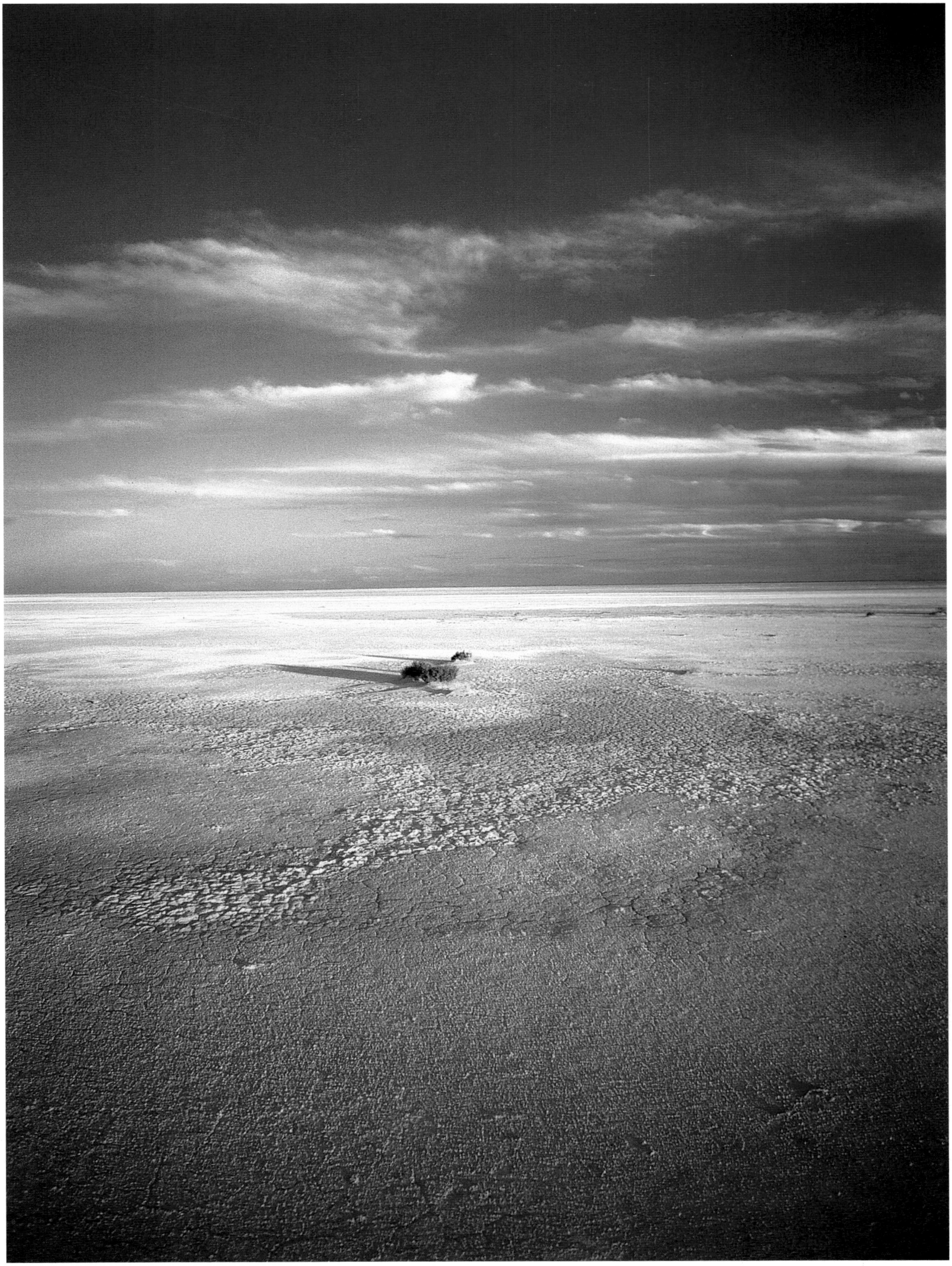

300 important rock engraving and cultural sites; it is also a sanctuary for emus, kangaroos and a wide range of wildlife. Other important Aboriginal locations include Uluru–Katatjuta National Park, the Flinders Ranges and the ancient Ewaninga rock carvings near Alice Springs.

The centre's extraordinary wildlife species, many of which descend from the prehistoric giant marsupials, are also long-term residents. This is the terrain of kangaroos, wallabies and other unique Australian marsupials; birds such as the flightless emu, the wedge-tailed eagle, galahs, cockatoos, budgerigars and members of the parrot family; and a wide range of snakes and lizards. The latter include the spiky and bizarre-looking thorny devil, as well as the perentie, a member of the goanna family that can be over 2m (6.5ft) long. A common sight in the outback's tropical fringe are termite mounds which dominate much of this northern landscape and are often up to 6m (20ft) high. Another indigenous mammal, the dingo, was the reason for the 5600km-long (3480 miles) 'Dog Fence' that stretched from the Darling Downs in Queensland to the Great Australian Bight in South Australia. This was the world's longest man-made barrier (twice as long as the Great Wall of China). Designed to keep dingoes out of the sheep-farming lands, fences are still maintained in Queensland at a high cost.

The arrival of the Europeans on the east coast in 1788 ultimately disrupted the long, harmonious Aboriginal and faunal occupation of the continent. As curiosity about the strange new land and its interior increased, explorers such as Thomas Mitchell, Edward John Eyre and Charles Sturt in the 1830s and 1840s laboured their way inland, battling against the heat, dust, attacks by the Aborigines, disease and even death, in search of farming land and what proved to be a mythical inland sea. John McDouall Stuart, the first person to cross the continent successfully from south to north (and return alive!), blazed an early 1860s trail that was followed by

Below There are few towns of any considerable size in the outback, but many thousands of people live on scattered and incredibly remote farming stations. Their isolation is relieved by aerial services such as the Royal Flying Doctor, and even flying shops.

Above As this sign reveals, Australia's Dog Fence runs for 5600km (3480 miles) across the continent and is designed to prevent native dogs, or dingoes, from straying into the sheep-farming land to the south. The dog fence is regularly checked by government inspectors.

(1142ft) sandstone monolith, with a circumference of 9km (5.6 miles), rises abruptly and dramatically from the plains, yet it is merely the tip of a 600 million-year-old underground 'mountain'. The nearby 30 or more rounded formations of Katatjuta (meaning 'many heads') are part of the same vast rock formation and, together, the sites are protected within Uluru–Katatjuta National Park, now under the custodianship of the local Pitjantjatjara and Yankuntjatjura Aboriginal people.

The Northern Territory contains many other geological wonders, including Kings Canyon in Watarrka National Park in the south, and the strangely balanced granite Devil's Marbles, south of Tennant Creek. The quartzite MacDonnell Ranges, near Alice Springs, encompass West MacDonnell National Park and the spectacular clefts of Standley Chasm, Simpsons Gap and Finke Gorge.

In South Australia, the low but craggy sandstone Flinders Ranges feature Wilpena Pound, a 10km-wide (6 miles) natural amphitheatre, while the nearby Gammon Ranges slightly to the north are another remarkable upland wilderness area. Isolated formations in the outback's east include the dramatic spires of New South Wales' Warrumbungle National Park and Queensland's 30km-long (19 miles) Carnarvon Gorge, with its vertical sandstone walls and Aboriginal art sites.

Until the arrival of Europeans in the late 18th century, Aborigines inhabited this unforgiving land with remarkable success for many thousands of years. Archaeological finds indicate that human beings had settled in Australia at least 40 000 years ago, but 50 000 years back is more likely. Despite a nomadic lifestyle that made buildings or permanent shelters redundant, Aboriginal people have left their mark in other ways. The outback contains many world-renowned cultural and archaeological locations that form a treasure-house of Aboriginal history. Mootwingee National Park in New South Wales, north-west of Wilcannia, for example, has over pastoralists in search of cattle-grazing land and prospectors seeking mineral riches. The Stuart Highway, which stretches from Adelaide in the south to Darwin in the north and provides a vital lifeline through the Centre, roughly follows the path of Stuart's epic trek – as does the 1870s Overland Telegraph Line to Darwin and the famous Ghan railway.

Many outback settlements owe their existence to these early pioneering journeys. Alice Springs, one of the Red Centre's largest towns with a population of 23 000, grew up around an Overland Telegraph station, as did Tennant Creek, also a very important gold-mining centre. The discovery of unimaginably rich lodes of silver, copper, lead and zinc in the 1870s and 1880s gave rise to the still thriving town of Broken Hill in New South Wales (population 25 000) and also Mount Isa (24 000) in Queensland. The presence of the world's most valuable opals led to the establishment of Coober Pedy in South Australia and New South Wales' Lightning Ridge and White Cliffs. The discovery in recent decades of natural gas at Moomba and of uranium, gold, silver and copper at Roxby Downs in South Australia helps to explain the presence of other towns and man-made structures in this most inhospitable region.

The Centre was opened up from the 1870s onwards by cattle farmers and drovers who created famous stock routes over vast distances for their thousands of cattle – for example, the Birdsville and Strzelecki tracks in Queensland and South Australia and the Canning Stock Route in Western Australia. Sheep farming, too, has played its part in European settlement, while tourism ensures the continuation of many small towns.

Outback wastelands have been the setting for far more mysterious activities. The vast 130 000 km² (50 180 sq miles) Woomera Prohibited Area in South Australia was used for rocket and missile testing from the 1950s to 1970s, and British nuclear devices were detonated at this region's Maralinga site during the 1950s. Although the radioactive area was supposedly 'cleaned up' after its abandonment in the 1960s, access is still restricted except to the Aboriginal owners of the land. Communication and transportation have always been vital in these extremely remote regions. Outback ingenuity in

conquering isolation and the 'tyranny of distance' is legendary. Long before roads existed, camels were used for exploration and ferrying supplies; wild descendants of these animals still roam the centre. Australia's international airline QANTAS (originally Queensland and Northern Territory Aerial Services Ltd) was founded in Winton, Queensland, in 1920, and the Royal Flying Doctor Service began at nearby Cloncurry in 1928. The latter still provides essential health services to many isolated settlements, operating from bases such as those at Broken Hill in New South Wales and Port Augusta in South Australia. Another remarkable invention is the School of the Air, which educates children through correspondence, radio and even by satellite.

While the vast majority of the Centre's non-Aboriginal population is scattered in small towns and remote rural properties, many indigenous Australians live a relatively traditional life on vast tracts of Aboriginal-owned land, much of which was 'returned' by the various state governments in the 1970s and 1980s. But whatever their origins, the people who inhabit this region do so warily – with a healthy sense of respect and an awareness of what little control they have over this harsh, unpredictable yet extraordinarily beautiful land.

Top A part of the woolshed at Jondaryan station in Queensland has been turned into a living museum with daily demonstrations of the art of shearing. Built in 1859, this large building is made of cedar and ironbark slabs. It once accommodated 88 shearers whose names can still be seen engraved on the rafter beams that were transported from England.

Above The Overland Telegraph Line was built between 1870 and 1872 to connect Adelaide to Darwin. It was the vision of Charles Todd, who also supervised its construction. The Alice Springs Telegraph Station operated for over 60 years. A number of the early stone buildings have now been restored and lie within an Aboriginal reserve.

Tennant Creek

Left Other than the important centres of Alice Springs in the Northern Territory, Broken Hill in New South Wales and Mount Isa in Queensland (which all have populations of around 25 000), the towns and villages of the Centre are mere dots on the map. In the Northern Territory, Katherine (population 10 000) is considered large, but most of these settlements rarely have more than 2 or 3 thousand people. One such town, Tennant Creek, began life as a repeater station for the Overland Telegraph Line that was constructed from Adelaide to Darwin in the early 1870s. Gold was then found in the area in 1932 and the settlement became the focus of Australia's 'Last Great Gold Rush'. This old gold stamp battery is a reminder of the days when gold was crushed in large quantities at Tennant Creek.

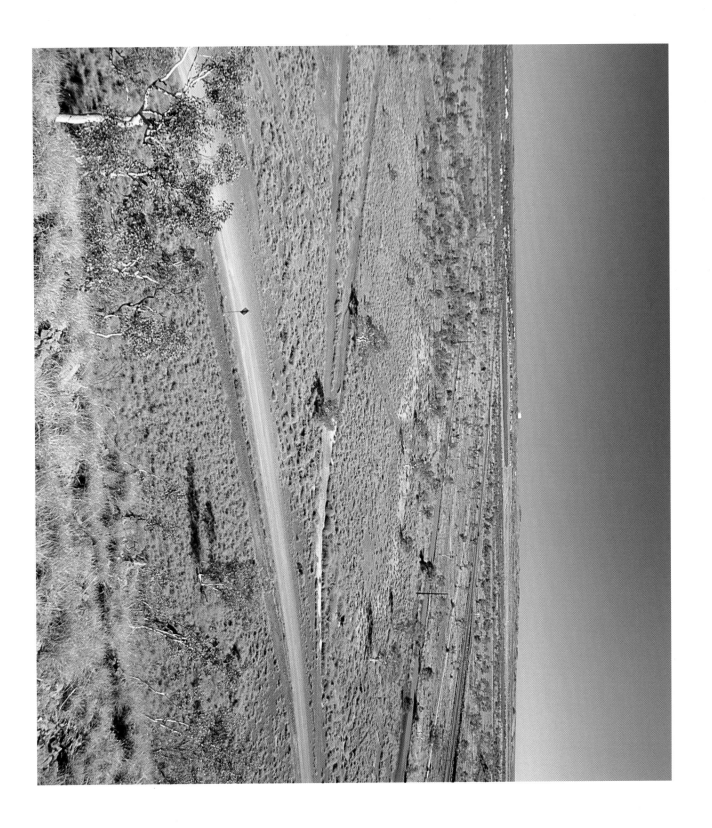

Above The original creek here was discovered by the explorer John McDouall Stuart in 1860, but very little traffic passed through the isolated Tennant Creek region until the coming of the Overland Telegraph Line a decade or so later. The town of Tennant Creek grew up on a plain about 10km (6 miles) south of the creek and is now the centre for a large cattle-farming region. The long history of gold, copper and silver mining continues with these metals still being extracted here, and the town also attracts its fair share of tourists. This view of Tennant Creek, from a rare hill outside the town, illustrates how flat, featureless and lightly vegetated this part of the Northern Territory is. The flora growing here, on the ubiquitous red outback earth, consists of little more than hardy grasses and shrubs, and scattered eucalyptus trees.

Devil's Marbles

Above, below left and below right The curious rocks known as the Devil's Marbles loom up on both sides of the highway to Alice Springs, 100km (62 miles) south of Tennant Creek in the Northern Territory. Once part of a large, single granite mass that has been eroded away over an estimated 1500 million years, these boulders ranging in size from massive to tiny now appear to balance precariously on one another. The rocks, weathered and rounded, are protected within the 1800ha (4448 acres) Devil's Marbles Conservation Reserve, where clumps of boulders are spread over a shallow valley and interspersed with typically resilient and drought-resistant outback vegetation.

Below Like the other famous rock formations of the centre such as Uluru and Katajuta, the Marbles appear to change colour at various stages throughout the day, according to the intensity and angle of the sun's rays. Sunset, when the light turns the rock a deep red colour, is considered to be the best time to view and photograph these spectacular

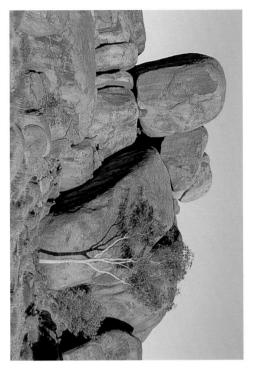

boulders. In Aboriginal mythology the Rainbow Serpent, believed to have laid the eggs, or 'marbles', is one of the important spirit beings that once roamed the continent, creating landforms like rivers, creeks and waterholes. Not surprisingly, the indigenous Australians regard this site as sacred and of great importance to their culture.

Kings Canyon

Above Kings Canyon is located in Watarrka National Park, at the western end of the relatively high plateau of the George Gill Range, and is about 345km (214 miles) north of Uluru and Katatjuta and formed from the same terracotta-coloured sandstone as its famous 'neighbours'. In addition to its rather spectacular canyon, Watarrka National Park is also famous for its permanent waterholes (a most unusual feature in this extremely arid part of the continent), many of which are surrounded by a fringe of palms, cycads, ferns and several other forms of lush vegetation. The sandstone from which the canyon is formed is extremely prone to erosion by wind and water, creating a range of weathered shapes in the rock. Varied colourings are an interesting feature of this stone – creams, ochres, browns and dark reds are common.

Right Instead of rising up from the surrounding plain like the previously mentioned scenic wonders, the cliffs of Kings Canyon plunge dramatically from the escarpment for about 300m (984ft) into the valley below, forming the Red Centre's deepest gorge. The national park was opened up to tourists only in the 1970s, but visitors can now take in the spectacular scenery from two perspectives: a walking track in the valley provides a good view of the gorge's sheer rock walls, and there is also a wonderful panorama of the canyon and surrounding countryside from the plateau above. Watarrka National Park's scenery is varied, however, and, in addition to the canyon itself, other landforms and geological features include red sandhills and the 'Lost City' – a series of strangely weathered sandstone outcrops that resemble domed buildings.

Aborigines in the outback

Left Although the 200 or so years since European settlement have disrupted Aboriginal life dramatically – by decimating the population, displacing indigenous Australians from their land, and imposing Western values – large numbers of Aborigines have returned to living a relatively traditional life. In the continent's far north, particularly in Arnhem Land, and around the central deserts of the Northern Territory, the native people have had much of their land returned by the government since the passing of the 1976 Aboriginal Land Rights Act and they have resumed, as far as possible, many of their old ways.

For 50 000 years, Australia's desert Aborigines, in particular, lived a nomadic life according to the seasons and the availability of food and water. Demonstrating a remarkable ability to survive in extraordinarily harsh conditions, they moved from place to place as waterholes dried up, fruits and berries came into season, and game became plentiful.

Although nowadays they are less dependent on the whims of climate and food sources and having a lifestyle that is supplemented by some modern conveniences, many central Australian Aboriginal people follow their traditional customs in the time-honoured way. There has also been a resurgence in arts and crafts like bark paintings, woven basketware and woodwork, with many of these beautiful and unique items finding their way into the galleries of Australian cities.

Above They may not look appealing to many people, but witchetty grubs are just one of the many forms of bush food that have long made up the diet of the Aboriginal people of the central Australian deserts. These large white grubs, the wood-boring larvae of certain moths and beetles, are dug out of the ground in great numbers and form what the Aboriginal people regard as a really delicious meal. Other highly sought-after 'bush tucker' includes honey ants that are also extracted from the ground, the large lizards known as goannas, snakes, edible berries, nuts and seeds from many species of trees and shrubs, and also several different birds. Other than hunting for larger animals such as kangaroos, which belonged strictly in the realm of male activities, the women traditionally foraged for most of the food for the Aboriginal communities – it is estimated that as much as 60 per cent of the daily food requirement was collected by women.

Somewhat surprisingly, a wide range of exotic native produce has become very popular in even the most upmarket city restaurants and hotels in recent years. It is not at all unusual to find interesting and tasty concoctions of crocodile, emu, kangaroo, buffalo, bunya nuts, wattle seeds and native fruits on many of these menus, while fish such as the barramundi and yabbies (freshwater crayfish) have long been popular with Australians of all persuasions.

Uluru

Left Uluru, located virtually at Australia's centre, rises dramatically from the plains. Along with Katatjuta, however, this is just the tip of a vast underground sandstone 'mountain' that is 600 million years old. The rock is 348m (1142ft) high and has an astonishing 9km (5.6 miles) circumference.

Below left Uluru is a very special place – its domination of the otherwise flat landscape is awesome – but to Aborigines this rock is of great spiritual significance. Though many tourists wish to climb to the top, there are two reasons to reconsider: the 1.6km (1 mile) climb is steep and dangerous, and indigenous Australians prefer that tourists do not trample over one of their most sacred sites.

Above right Depending on the time of day, the colour of Uluru's sandstone walls appears to change from pale mauves, pinks and blues to brown, a fiery red, and this warm orange.

Right Visitors who do not climb Uluru can take an Aboriginal-guided walk around a section of the base, where paintings and unusual perspectives, such as this, are revealed.

Opposite From a distance Uluru, located in Uluru–Katatjuta National Park, which is under the custodianship of the local Aborigines and a designated World Heritage site, appears to have a smooth surface. A close-up inspection, however, shows deep gullies carved in the sandstone by the erosive forces of wind and water over millions of years.

Katatjuta

Left Fifty kilometres (31 miles) from Uluru, Katatjuta, formerly known as the Olgas, rises from the same subterranean sandstone block as its more famous cousin. But unlike Uluru, Katatjuta is a series of rounded formations that seem less impressive at first glance. At the peak of Mount Olga, however, these striated and weathered domes rise to 200m (656ft) higher than Uluru and the many gorges, caves and curious formations are just as intriguing as anything that Uluru has to offer.

Above and below Appropriately for this phenomenon of 36 domes, the name Katatjuta means 'many heads' in the Aboriginal language. The steep-sided rocks cover an area of 3500ha (8649 acres) that is worth exploring: the region is home to 150 bird species, kangaroos, and the large perentie lizard. Although the Red Centre is dry for most of the year, rain does fall on occasions, producing surprises like these white and yellow wildflowers among the hardy shrubs and grasses.

Survival in the Centre

Top There are several different reasons why towns in the centre of Australia came into existence: for Kalgoorlie it was the 'big strike' of 1893. The gold rush brought thousands of prospectors to this arid region where dust storms and the harsh heat make life tough. The awnings of the buildings on this revitalised street are a common feature of many outback towns. They stretch out over the pavements to protect shop merchandise and pedestrians from the relentless sun.

Above left Because of the incredible distances between towns, a petrol station is an oasis to the long-distance traveller. This one at Marree lies conveniently at the junction of the Birdsville and Oodnadatta tracks.

Above The 'one pub town' is the description of many tiny outback settlements like William Creek. This is the closest town to Lake Eyre and came to life during the building of the Overland Telegraph Line.

Above Quorn came into existence when railway lines began to cross the country. It was an important junction between Perth, Broken Hill, Alice Springs and Adelaide. Today the Pichi Richi Railway Preservation Society maintains this beautiful, restored station and operates special trips on narrow-gauge trains. One active line, though, considered to be the oldest intact railway system in the world, still operates from Quorn to Port Augusta, carrying ore from the mines in the north.

Above When copper and lead were found in the district, convicts were sent in to help build the township of Northampton. It became a bustling supply centre for the Geraldine Mines in the 1850s, but today the town only services nearby cattle and sheep stations. Many of the old buildings have been restored, including the Warribanno Chimney built in 1851. This wide, carved street scene reflects the quiet, rural and casual atmosphere found in many outback towns.

Life on the road

Opposite The wide, unsealed Gibb River Road runs for 670km (416 miles) across vast tracts of rolling landscape and is used to reach areas inaccessible by other means of transport. These roads of fine red dust are sometimes the only access to and from districts in the centre. Many roads began when settlers, following routes discovered by explorers, travelled inland to set up vast stations. The roads grew from these humble beginnings to vital links between towns all over the continent.

Above and left In these vast outback terrains the stations are usually unfenced and passing motorists need to be wary of wandering cattle as well as the wildlife which can suddenly appear on the horizon. Another hazard is the road trains that thunder along the isolated roads kicking up dust and obstructing vision. These road trains carry stock and supplies between the scattered populations of the outback and the capital cities. Because of the lack of navigable rivers and canals in the Centre and the difficulty of supplying rail services to such isolated places, road trains have become, in many instances, the only means of freight transport. These articulated lorries, consisting of a prime mover and one or more trailers, very often travel in groups. In the last century, particularly since World War II, resources have been directed towards road safety, with continual sealing, building and maintenance of roads by the governments of Australia. Of the estimated 800 000km (500 000 miles) of recognised roads open to general traffic throughout the continent, just under two-fifths are sealed with either bitumen, concrete, gravel or other improved surface.

Coober Pedy

Above For many residents of Coober Pedy, an opal-mining settlement, escape from the heat has created unusual living conditions. Beneath the arid country, cool homes are dug with picks and shovels. These unique underground homes are equipped with modern conveniences and are ideal to escape the fierce temperatures which often exceed 40°C (104°F). The town's name is apt, as it means 'hole in the ground', or more colloquially 'white feller's burrow', in the local Aboriginal dialect.

Right Large mounds of dirt scatter the landscape of Coober Pedy. These banks of pale mullock are the result of opal field diggings. Opals were first discovered in the area in 1911 but new veins came to light in the 1960s and saw hundreds of miners flocking to the area in the hope of striking it rich. Some of the opal veins lie 30m (98ft) below the surface and long shafts are sunk into the layers of sandstone to reach them. Lying 931km (579 miles) north-west of Adelaide, and west of Lake Eyre, in the arid centre of South Australia, Coober Pedy is an isolated settlement. The town was originally known as the Stuart Range Opal Field because it is located in the barren Stuart Range.

Below The township of Coober Pedy has an air-conditioned motel, shops and other conveniences, but many miners and their families prefer to live underground. The dug-outs are elaborate and even churches and shops are built into the red earth. Air and some natural light find their way into the residences via strategically placed shafts. The decor of the underground dwellings reflects the sense of humour of their eccentric owners and the multicultured make-up of the population. The food outlets in the area cater for the different cuisines of the locals.

A varied desert terrain

Above Although all arid and inhospitable, Australia's desert regions present a variety of terrains. The Strzelecki Desert in South Australia contains red sand and rock that somehow supports trees and shrubs.

Below Enormous tracts of wind-sculpted sand make up much of the central deserts. The large Koonchera Dune, again in the outback of South Australia, glows with golden light at dawn.

Left Stretching for over 150 000km² (57 900 sq miles) across the Red Centre, the Simpson Desert is characterised by its tall sand dunes that run in parallel lines for up to 200km (124 miles). Even here, though, trees like the drought-resistant gidgee still manage to thrive.

Below Although now crossed by vehicle tracks, the Sturts Stony Desert remains as forbidding and barren as when the first downcast explorers attempted to traverse this plain of iron-stained rocks during the 1840s.

The Flinders Ranges

Left *The Flinders Ranges are one of Australia's major mountain chains. Around the settlement of Arkaroola there is some spectacular semiarid scenery that is related to indigenous legend. According to Aboriginal beliefs, the Dreamtime serpent Arkaroo carved out gorges and riverbeds as it slithered its way to drink from nearby lakes. Despite the lack of rainfall and fertile soil, these grasstrees (xanthorrhoeas) manage to grow out of what is little more than bare rock.*

Right *The Flinders Ranges are now a series of craggy but low hills, and it is hard to imagine that this was once a lofty mountain range on a Himalayan scale. The once high peaks have been eroded over millions of years and the highest point is now only 1200m (3937ft). The red sandstone rocks of the northern Flinders Ranges contain minerals, such as copper ore, that were exploited in the last century. Mines, smelters and townships once thrived here despite heat, isolation, inhospitable terrain and harsh living conditions, and many ruins still remain today.*

Below *Once a sheep station, the Arkaroola area is now a privately owned wildlife sanctuary. Nature lovers are drawn to Arkaroola and the nearby Gammon Ranges National Park by the scenery, excellent bush-walking and wildlife in the form of wallabies, kangaroos, emus and other unique birdlife. The area is rich in Aboriginal paintings, etchings and burial sites. This panorama provides a typical glimpse of the area – grasstrees, rocks and peaks, with semiarid plains in the distance.*

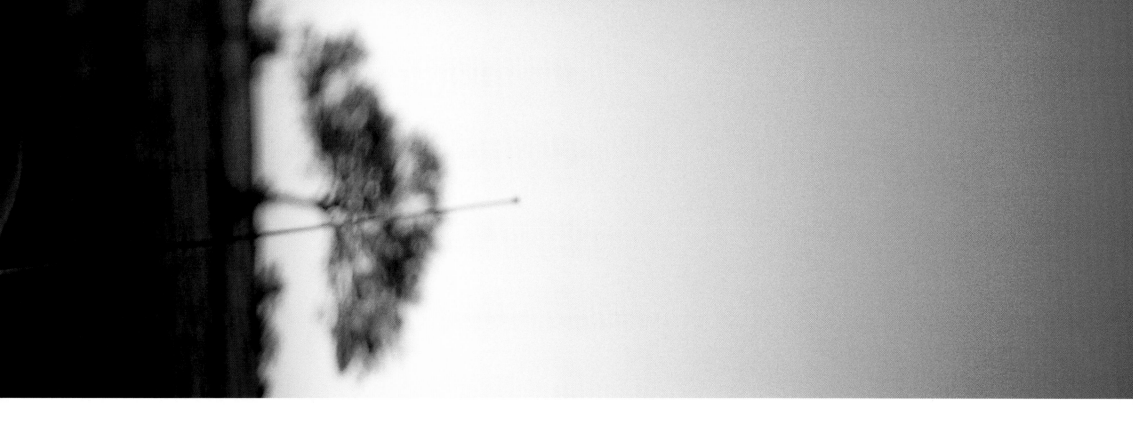

Resilient people of the outback

Left Since its settlement in the post-1860s period, the outback has produced some remarkably hardy people. Although modern life is more comfortable, these Australians have always coped with isolation, heat, lack of water and hardships beyond the imagination of most city dwellers. The tradition of the tough, taciturn but humorous bushman was born here – an image that persists, even if the nation is essentially a land of city and coastal dwellers. Australia's 'cowboys' – men and women who spend days in the saddle – are very much a part of this tradition.

Above The tiny outback South Australian settlement of Innamincka has had a fascinating history: Explorers like Charles Sturt explored this very remote area from the 1840s onwards, and the region is closely linked to the tragic Burke and Wills expedition of 1860–61 when the team's leaders perished in this inhospitable terrain. Innamincka also has long links with the cattle industry; last century it became an important droving centre for stockmen taking cattle from Queensland to the markets in Adelaide. The connection endures to this day and the region is home to hardy cattle and their equally resilient drovers and stockmen.

Below The Queensland town of Birdsville is a legend. Located in Channel Country where the deserts break up into alternately dry and filled rivers and lakes, it began life as an outpost on the famous cattle stock route, the Birdsville Track. Although home to just a few hundred people, the village hosts up to 5 thousand for the annual Birdsville Races. After watching horses gallop around the grassless course, visitors and locals alike throng to the pub to make merry, consume enormous quantities of beer, and enjoy the local colour and entertainment.

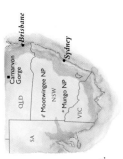

Carnarvon Gorge

Previous pages Although it is situated quite far inland, the dramatic 30km-long (19 miles) Carnarvon Gorge in outback Queensland is also an integral part of the Great Dividing Range that is otherwise located much further to the east of the continent. Protected within the confines of the beautiful and scenic Carnarvon National Park, the gorge's sheer 200m-high (656ft) pale sandstone walls and the densely wooded valley below are home to a fantastic and varied range of wildlife, including grey kangaroos, several varieties of wallabies, platypuses, snakes, water dragons, and many bird species. The fertile creek-lined gorge, despite its location in a very dry plateau region, supports some extraordinarily lush vegetation, with cabbage palms, tree ferns, cycads, mosses and ferns all thriving here. There are more than 50 Aboriginal art sites within the national park itself, most of which are stencils of hands, feet and items such as boomerangs, although paintings and engravings also feature on the sandstone rock.

Mootwingee National Park

Above In the remote far west of New South Wales, Mootwingee National Park is particularly rich in Aboriginal history and culture – many of the sandstone rocks here are adorned with ancient artwork such as these hand stencils.

Below Aboriginal people of the past regularly visited the Mootwingee area's rock shelters and semipermanent waterholes, and evidence of their long occupation remains in over 300 rock art sites. This petroglyph depicts a highly stylised but still recognisable kangaroo.

Right This national park's rugged terrain is characterised by narrow gorges, large expanses of brown sandstone rocks, and hardy vegetation such as river red gums, mulga trees and cypress pines.

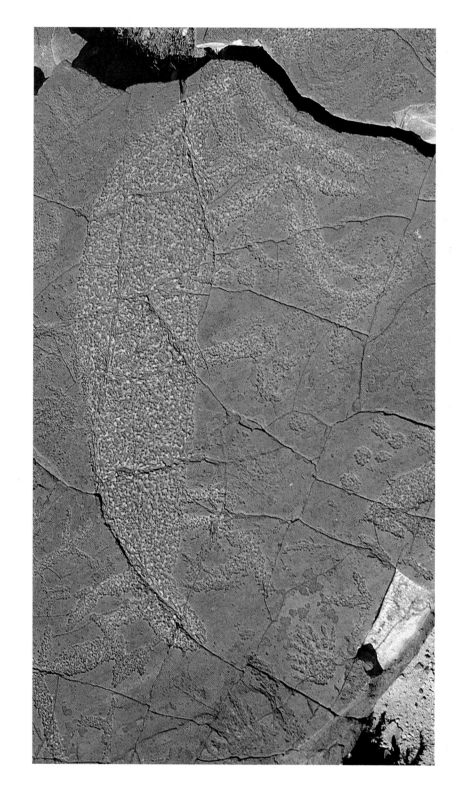

Mungo National Park

Above Mungo National Park, the location of a series of freshwater lakes until 15 000 years ago, is now a vast area of incredibly arid sandy country. The national park is included in the Willandra Lakes World Heritage region, listed both for its geographical features and its record of unimaginably long Aboriginal occupation. Internationally recognised for its archaeological importance, it contains the world's oldest known cremation site, and human and tool remains as much as 40 000 years old. Although extremely remote — in the far south-west of New South Wales and reached by a road that becomes impassable after rain — the park still receives around 12 000 intrigued visitors each year.

Left The park's most famous geological feature is a 25km-long (16 miles) crescent-shaped lunette or dune, the 'Walls of China', that follows Lake Mungo's northern and eastern shores. Composed of sand and clay from the dry lakebed, this phenomenon was created initially by the effects of the westerly winds that blew the deposits onto the lakeside. The material then solidified, and the walls now contain multicoloured layers that have become eroded into strange shapes by the effects of wind and water over aeons of time. These pillars and gullies are of far more significance, however, than merely as curious landforms. The layers of clay and sand have become a sort of weather gauge that has recorded changes in climate — from wet to dry, and encompassing the period when the lake was full of water, over a period of 15 000–30 000 years — and that has excited the interest of archaeologists throughout the world.

The SOUTH

RUGGED EDGES MEET COOLER CLIMES

Australia's cool, damp South – encompassing Victoria, Tasmania and a small portion of South Australia – presents a marked contrast to the more northerly areas of the continent. The climate here, affected by cool Southern Ocean breezes and even chilly Antarctic winds, is much more temperate, and winter snowfalls are common on the highlands. The land is also extremely varied, ranging from forests to lakes and dunes along the coast to the surprisingly cold mountains.

The 'high country' of north-eastern Victoria is the tail end of the Great Dividing Range, which snakes its way down the continent's eastern fringe. Much of this region, covered in snow from June to September and popular with skiers, is taken up by the 6500km^2 (2509 sq miles) Alpine National Park. Encompassing the lofty (by Australian standards) heights of 1986m-high (6516ft) Mount Bogong (Victoria's tallest peak), Mount Buller and Mount Hotham, the park also features high plains and alpine vegetation with many wildflowers and snow gums. Wildlife includes the rare mountain pygmy possum, a unique alpine marsupial.

This high region was important for Aboriginal food-gathering in days past but, apart from tourism, the upland plains are now used mainly for summer cattle grazing. Further south, Baw Baw National Park's granite plateau supports subalpine vegetation and open forest, and is the home of the endangered Leadbeater's possum. To the west, the stark Grampians form an important Aboriginal and natural reserve.

Many paintings adorn the walls of the caves and shelters, and the park also contains many rare wildflowers and over 200 bird species, the highlights of which are wedge-tailed eagles and peregrine falcons.

Some of Australia's most impressive mountain scenery, however, is on the island state of Tasmania. Until the maritime explorations of George Bass and Matthew Flinders took place in 1798, Tasmania – then known as Van Diemen's Land – was believed to be part of the mainland. The wild winds and waters of the Bass Strait have claimed many ships, but the region has abundant wildlife: seals, whales and the rare Cape Barren goose which is found on King and Flinders islands. These isles are also a nesting site for migratory short-tailed shearwaters or muttonbirds.

Tasmania's capital, Hobart, became the nation's third major settlement in 1804 when the town was founded as a penal colony. Port Arthur, which followed in 1830, was particularly suitable for this purpose, located as it was on the then remote Tasman Peninsula, with its rugged coastline and narrow entrance point. The European occupation of Tasmania, however, brought about one of the ugliest chapters in the colony's history. The indigenous population was subject to vast brutalisation until, in 1833, the only small band of surviving Aborigines was banished to Flinders Island. Only a handful remained by the 1840s.

Left Victoria's Great Ocean Road, between Torquay and Port Fairy, forms Australia's most scenic driving route. This 300km-long (186 miles) road, completed in 1932, hugs the Southern Ocean coastline and presents some spectacular vistas. The towering Twelve Apostles, vast chunks of limestone that have become separated from the mainland by the forces of erosion, are the region's most famous natural formations.

Previous pages Although most people imagine Australia as a land of desert, tropics and coastline, the island continent is more varied in its terrain and climate. In the south-east the peaks of the Great Dividing Range reach heights of over 2000m (6562ft), and the cool winter climate means that snow covers these ranges for several months of the year. Victoria's Alpine National Park is one such chilly upland area.

Above South Australia's Kangaroo Island is renowned for its rugged coastline and weathered granite, which takes on a particularly smooth appearance at Remarkable Rocks on the wind-battered south coast.

Below Australia's best known carnivorous marsupial is the Tasmanian devil. Found only in the island state, the devil has particularly sharp claws and teeth and grows to around 55–60cm (22–24in) in length.

Above In one of the craters of a long-extinct volcano, Blue Lake, near Mount Gambier in South Australia, mysteriously changes colour from grey to this brilliant blue for a few months of each year.

Right Lake Bonney was once the site of a failed attempt to break the world water-speed record. In 1964 Donald Campbell reached the amazing speed of 347.5km/h (215.9 mph) here.

Tasmania presents one of Australia's most spectacular natural environments. In the south and west, the national parks of Cradle Mountain–Lake St Clair, Franklin–Gordon Wild Rivers and the Southwest combine to form a 1.4 million-hectare (3.5 million acres) World Heritage region. This cool-temperate wilderness consists of lakes, rivers, moors, a formidable coastline, rugged peaks – including Mount Ossa, the state's highest point at 1617m (5305ft), and Frenchmans Cap – and some remarkable vegetation. Alpine plants and grasses, snow gums, wildflowers, pandanus, button grass and temperate rainforest all flourish here.

The region's waterways were the focus of enormous controversy during the early 1980s when hydro-electric power schemes threatened the wilderness. 'Progress' was eventually halted in the name of conservation and much of the island's southern region still supports the famous tall-growing Tasmanian trees such as the Antarctic beech, the mountain ash and the Huon pine. The equally rich wildlife includes platypus, wombat and wallaby communities, as well as some animals that are unique to the island. The striped Tasmanian tiger (thylacine) is by now probably extinct, but another carnivorous marsupial – the fierce little Tasmanian devil – is still relatively common here.

There are several other superb natural regions on this remarkable island. East-coast Freycinet National Park is well known for its white, sandy beaches and granite headlands,

while the forested plateau of Mount Field National Park is a popular skiing venue. Human beings have made rather less of an impact on Tasmania's wild uplands than in many other parts of Australia, but tin, copper and zinc mining in the west as well as land clearing for sheep and cattle farming have, inevitably, left their mark on this very special environment.

Victoria's Phillip Island is another offshore wildlife sanctuary. This island is the province of kangaroos, fur seals and seabirds

such as pelicans and mutton-birds. In a bid to boost koala colonies, these animals have recently been introduced to the island sanctuary. The island was originally inhabited by Aborigines, followed by early 1800s sealers and whalers, but most of today's visitors are tourists who flock to see the nightly 'parade' of tiny fairy penguins from the sea to their burrows.

The coastline of the South's mainland, despite being well populated, encompasses many unspoilt natural wonders. In the far east are the lakes, islands, forests and dunes of Crojingolong National Park, and the Gippsland Lakes – a maze of waterways and sandy coast. Lakes and dunes also predominate in South Australia's Coorong National Park, as well as a narrow 145km-long (90 miles) lagoon and the Younghusband Peninsula. There are around 400 bird species here, including cormorants, ibises and a large pelican colony. The area was once frequented by Aboriginal people, who have left their mark in the form of food middens.

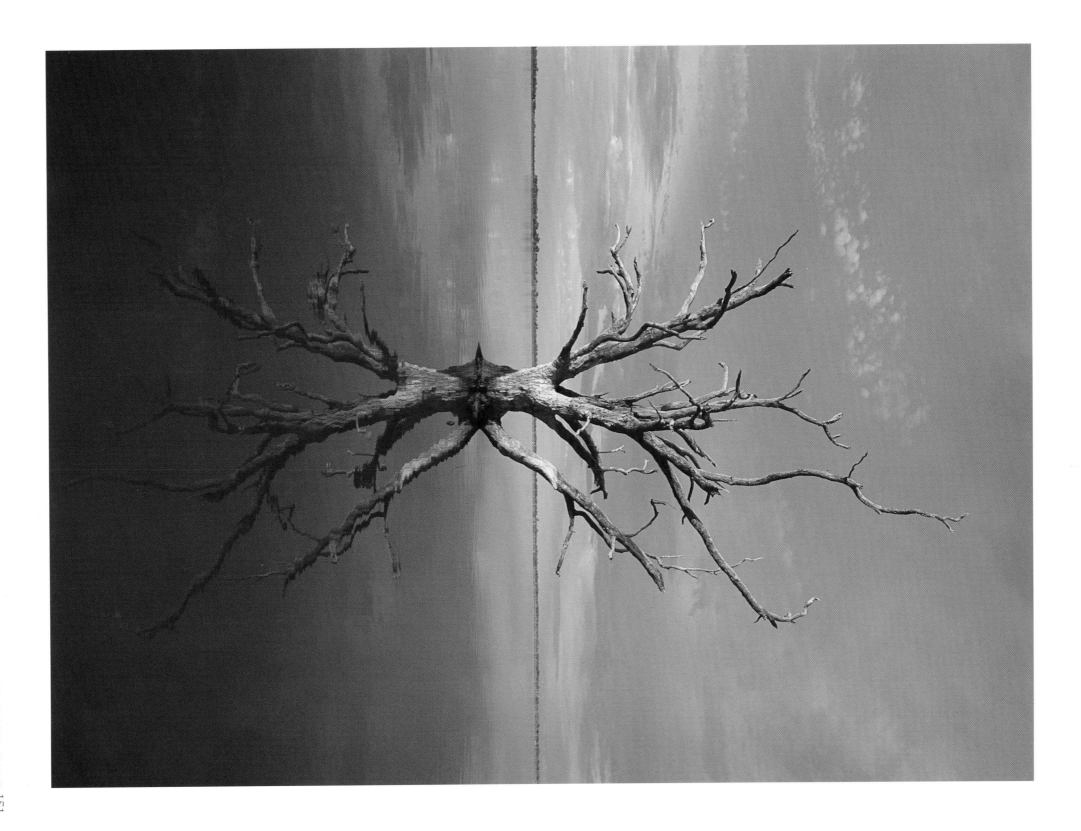

Left The South Australian capital of Adelaide is a most attractive city, and unusual in that it was carefully planned from its beginnings in 1836. Surrounded by parkland, bisected by the River Torrens, and with an orderly grid of central city streets, Adelaide was the vision of surveyor Colonel William Light. The city's one million residents enjoy a Mediterranean-style climate and a relatively peaceful lifestyle.

This view looks south towards the city centre, with St Peters Cathedral (1869) on the left, the Adelaide Oval cricket ground to the right, and the white roofs of the Adelaide Festival Centre in the distance. This latter building is the focus for the internationally acclaimed biennial Arts Festival. In the far distance are the cool, wooded Adelaide Hills, with their bushland, gardens, and German culture and heritage.

Dramatic coastal scenery is found in Victoria's Wilsons Promontory National Park, a rugged granite peninsula that forms the mainland's most southerly point, and in the cliffs and extraordinary offshore formations of the limestone Port Campbell region further west. Along this section of the coastline, and bearing descriptive names such as the 'Twelve Apostles' and 'London Bridge', are wind- and wave-eroded outcrops which once formed part of the mainland. This spectacular but treacherous stretch, known as the 'Shipwreck Coast', is also a nesting place for muttonbirds. Inland, the damp, forested Otway Ranges support tree ferns, platypuses and ringtail possums. Still further west lie the towns and fishing centres of Warrnambool, Port Fairy and Portland, which was a sealing station in the 1830s.

In South Australia, the beautiful coastline curves past the crayfishing town of Robe, the Younghusband Peninsula and Coorong National Park to the Fleurieu Peninsula. Now a

The Coorong National Park adjoins Lake Alexandrina and Lake Albert, where the nation's longest river, the Murray, reaches the sea after its 2500km (1554 miles) journey from the New South Wales Snowy Mountains. The Murray River marks much of the New South Wales–Victoria border, and it spawned major 19th-century river ports such as Echuca, Swan Hill and Mildura. Paddle-steamers, such as the *Philadelphia* made famous by the television series *All the Rivers Run*, still cruise the Murray. To catch one is an idyllic way to explore the region and the prolific birdlife along the river, the banks of which are dominated by magnificent river red gums. The Murray enters South Australia near the heavily irrigated Renmark wine and citrus fruit-growing region. This 1880s watering scheme still irrigates large tracts of otherwise arid land, but increasing salinity has caused rather severe environmental problems. The Riverland once sustained large Aboriginal communities and evidence of their long occupation of this area – shell middens, artefacts and burial sites – still remains.

Located off the coast of South Australia, Kangaroo Island, the nation's second-largest island (145km, or 90 miles, long and 60km, or 37 miles, wide) is very aptly named. This island, and particularly Flinders Chase National Park, forms a notable wildlife sanctuary where kangaroos, tammar wallabies, echidnas, New Zealand fur seals, albatrosses and fairy penguins thrive. Emus and koalas, introduced from the mainland, also flourish here but the island is most important for its rare Australian sea-lion colony. The flora, too, is really quite exceptional – there are more than 50 species of orchids, as well as extensive heathland and eucalypt forests. Kangaroo Island features dramatic granite cliffs, strangely shaped rocks and limestone caves, and it is also historically significant; the town of Kingscote was South Australia's first official settlement.

popular holiday region consisting of small towns, wineries and nature reserves, this peninsula's cliff- and beach-dotted coast was once an important Aboriginal hunting and camping ground.

Neighbouring Gulf St Vincent was the entry point for Adelaide's early European settlers, who first arrived in 1836. The South Australian capital was founded by free settlers and Adelaide prides itself on its convict-less history. Surrounded by the gentle Adelaide Hills and the gulf, this is perhaps the nation's most attractive capital. Adelaide has a multicultural population of just over a million and the city has gained a reputation as an important centre for the arts.

West of Adelaide, across Gulf St Vincent, the Yorke Peninsula's rich lodes of copper were once heavily mined, but this region is now known for its cereal crops — as is the Eyre Peninsula, beyond the inlet of Spencer Gulf, and the industrial centres of Port Pirie, Port Augusta and Whyalla, which are situated on the peninsula's east coast. The Eyre also has quite a large tuna and abalone fishing industry based at Port Lincoln, while some of the gulf's other occupants are dolphins and sea lions, Cape Barren geese and also the fearsome great white shark.

Some of the nation's most important wine-growing areas are located in South Australia, where a large percentage of Australia's grape production is harvested. Settled initially by German immigrants, the lovely rolling hills and vales of the Barossa Valley produce superb vintages, as does the nearby Clare Valley.

Beyond the remote Nuyts Archipelago (first charted by Pieter Nuijts aboard the Dutch ship *Gulden Zeepaard* in 1627 and believed to have been the inspiration for Jonathan Swift's 'Lilliput'), the coastline changes dramatically to encompass the sheer Nullarbor cliffs that plunge into the Southern Ocean. From here, the barren Nullarbor Plain stretches interminably west, and to the north are the vast South Australian deserts that are occupied only by isolated Aboriginal communities.

The state's south-east offers ancient wonders in the shape of Mount Gambier's limestone caves and the volcanic lakes, including the famous Blue Lake, the main crater of Mount Gambier's four, and the Victoria Fossil Cave near Naracoorte. This cave, a relatively recent addition to Australia's World Heritage list, revealed the bones of prehistoric creatures in 1969 and is now widely regarded as one of the world's most important fossil sites.

Until the post-1820s exploration of the interior, travel to the continent's south was always by sea — Victoria's capital city of Melbourne, for example, was founded in 1835 by pioneers who had sailed there from Tasmania. Located beside the Yarra River on the vast Port Phillip Bay, Melbourne is Australia's most European-style and refined capital, with a culturally mixed population of over three million. The city is near some delightful natural environments: for example, the Dandenong Ranges, with their eucalypt woodlands, fern gullies, orchids and flamboyant lyrebirds, form a flora and wildlife sanctuary that is rare so close to a major city.

Much of Victoria's well-populated interior contains fertile agricultural land, but a tract of semidesert — featuring the dry lakes and shrubby mallee forest (home to the rare mallee fowl) of Wyperfeld National Park — creates a striking contrast to this in the far north-west. Mineral riches include coal in the Latrobe Valley and oil and gas in the Bass Strait, but gold once dominated Victorian life. The state boomed after the metal's discovery north-west of Melbourne in the 1850s, and settlements such as Ballarat and Bendigo contain many grand buildings as reminders of their mining heyday — a time when the goldfields created extraordinary wealth and placed the southern city of Melbourne firmly on the map.

Left and above Melbourne, Australia's second-largest city with a population of over three million, was founded in the 1830s, long after Sydney. Despite the late start, Melbourne competed fiercely with its northern rival for the title of the nation's premier city and it still contains many grand buildings from the mid- to late-1800s. This aerial shot (left) takes in the Yarra River, the Royal Botanic Gardens and Government House, and the centre's tall buildings, while a closer view of the city skyline and Yarra (above) is seen from the river's south bank.

Croajingolong National Park

Left The 86 000ha (212 506 acres) Croajingolong National Park situated in Victoria preserves a lovely coastal region of rivers, lakes, forest, islands, beaches and sand dunes. There are some extensive beaches here, as well as the large Mallacoota Inlet which is fed by a dozen or so rivers and streams. These dunes are near historic Point Hicks, the site of a solar-powered lighthouse and an obelisk that records Captain Cook's first sighting of Australia from the Endeavour, offshore from this point in April 1770. The name of Croajingolong is believed to be Aboriginal for 'looking eastwards' or 'go east'.

Below Croajingolong National Park extends for around 100km (62 miles) along this remote corner of the Victorian coast and offers varied scenery. In addition to the sandy beaches and large dune system, much of which is littered with driftwood and dead trees, the park is characterised by a wide range of flora. The river banks are clad in dense forests of trees such as the swamp paperbark, while rainforest gullies support ferns, orchids and exotic trees. There is also abundant birdlife, with around one-third of Australia's bird species having been recorded here. Pelicans, black swans, sea eagles and cormorants are found in the vicinity of Mallacoota Inlet and the area's lakes, while the eucalypt forests are inhabited by kookaburras, spectacular lyrebirds and eastern whipbirds – the later being famous for their strange whipcrack-like call.

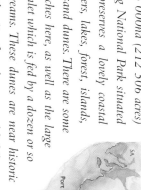

Mount Buffalo National Park

Above The 31 000ha (76 601 acres) Mount Buffalo National Park, was established way back in 1898 to preserve a region of superbly wild and rugged mountain terrain that is part of the Great Dividing Range. Mount Buffalo itself is a 35km² (13.5 sq miles), lightly vegetated granite plateau that reaches a height of 1723m (5653ft) at the rock pyramid known as The Horn, but below these rocky heights the slopes are heavily forested with eucalyptus and wattle trees. The intrepid explorers Hume and Hovell passed through this region in 1824 and named the mountain for its humped, buffalo-like shape.

This national park is famed for its spectacular views – such as this of The Gorge, a weathered granite outcrop, in the early morning. The rock's 300m-high (984ft) walls are often dotted with experienced rock climbers, while the less adventurous can walk to the edge for a superb panorama of the surrounding hills, ridges and valleys.

Right Non-Australians are often quite surprised to learn that skiing is a major winter activity (predominantly in the months of June to September) in the continent's south-east. There are several ski runs, lifts and resorts in the highlands of southern New South Wales, Tasmania, and here in the Victorian Alps, as well as some excellent cross-country skiing through totally unpopulated terrain.

Skiing has been popular in Australia since the 1860s, and the nation even makes a claim to having the world's first ski club – formed at the New South Wales village of Kiandra in 1870. The country's first ski lift was opened at Mount Buffalo in the 1940s and today the area's relatively easy slopes and good facilities make it popular with beginners and families. Many of these skiers come from Melbourne – just a three-hour drive away. This Mount Buffalo panorama takes in snow-covered, tree-dotted slopes and lines of ridge tops that stretch to the horizon.

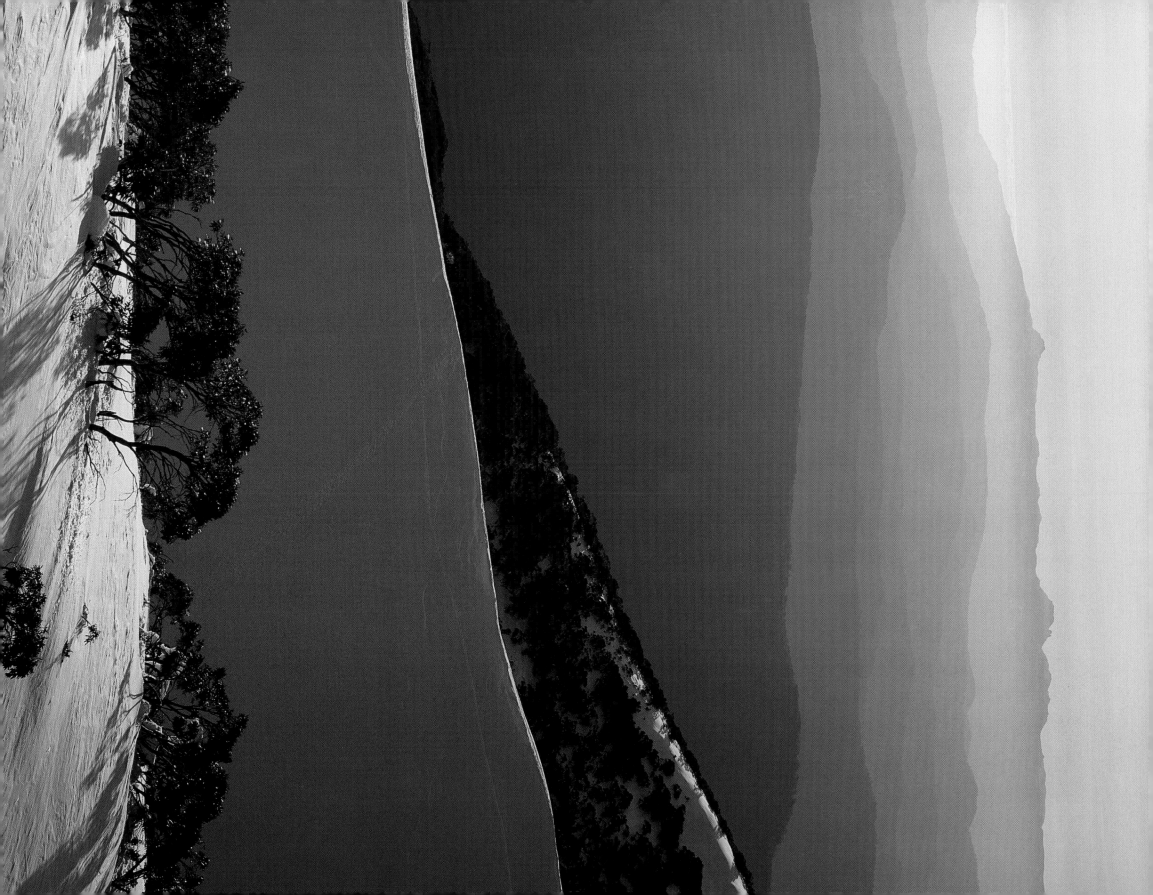

Alpine National Park

Above To the south and east of Mount Buffalo, the Alpine National Park takes up quite a large portion of eastern Victoria and forms the state's largest reserve. At 646 000ha (1.6 million acres), this region of high peaks and awesome mountain scenery is a remarkable upland wilderness where very few (other than skiers) walkers and rock climbers venture. In times long past, the area was an important ceremonial and food-gathering ground for Aboriginal people, who came particularly for the Bogong moths that flock here in their millions each summer.

The Alpine National Park encompasses Victoria's highest peak, 1986m-high (6516ft) Mount Bogong, and several other high summits such as Mount Buller and Mount Hotham. These heights may seem quite modest but Australia, the world's flattest continent, possesses no point higher than just over 2220m (7284ft). The Victorian peaks and high plateaus are snow-covered for several months of the year and very little vegetation, other than heath, grasses and trees like this exceptionally hardy but wind-blasted snow gum, can survive here.

Left In summer and the warmer months of the year, the Alpine National Park takes on a very different guise. Once the snow has melted the high plains become, as they have since the 1850s, a grazing ground for cattle. Although much of the grazing land now falls within the national park, the area's cattlemen have been allowed to continue this long tradition. In spring and early summer, a blaze of colourful wildflowers covers these plains and the eucalypt-clad lower slopes of the peaks. The area's wildlife includes the rare and possibly endangered mountain pygmy possum. This delightful little marsupial, just 10–12cm (4–5in) long and well adapted to life above the snow line, is found only around Mount Hotham and a couple of other small, isolated areas of the Australian Alps.

Other sections of the vast Alpine National Park, which incorporated three already protected areas in 1989, include part of the rugged Snowy River valley, and the upper reaches of the Murray, Australia's longest river. There are several other rare or endangered animal species here, and the vegetation includes a number of plants that are found nowhere else.

Dandenong Ranges National Park

Above Only 50km (31 miles) east of the city, the Dandenong Ranges, a region of hills, eucalypt forests and orchid-filled gullies, form one of Melbourne's most popular recreation areas. These magnificent 90m-high (295ft) mountain ash trees are in the Sherbrooke Forest, part of the Dandenong Ranges National Park. Despite the name, this tree is a form of eucalyptus and the world's tallest-growing hardwood.

Right The Dandenong National Park comprises three areas of superb forest country – including the Ferntree Gully park, the oldest of the three reserves – that are blessed with high rainfall. Featuring forests of tree ferns, mosses and other vegetation, the Ferntree Gully park forms a striking contrast to the park's tall eucalypt, sassafras and myrtle beech forests. Other attractions of the Dandenong Ranges include the views from Mount Dandenong, and the historic Puffing Billy steam train that winds its way through the forest on 13km (8 miles) of track. There are many gardens such as this (right) which are open to the public.

Below The Dandenong region is famous for its parks and gardens, including the rhododendron, camellia and azalea reserve at Olinda. Imported plants feature in English-style gardens, where leaves carpet the ground in autumn and create a rather atypical Australian scene.

The Grampians (Gariwerd) National Park

Above Now supplemented by its Aboriginal name, the Grampians (Gariwerd) National Park forms the westernmost extension of the Great Dividing Range. It is concentrated around the peaks and ridges of the Grampian mountains that fall to the valleys in steep, eroded escarpments and cliffs. The area was declared a national park in 1984 and is a haven for bushwalkers, rock climbers and birdwatchers—there are over 200 species of birds here. This spectacular view is from Mount William, the park's highest point at 1170m (3839ft). The summit also features a memorial to Sir Thomas Mitchell who explored this region in 1836 and named the area after the peaks of his native Scotland.

Left This national park is known for its ancient rock shelters and formations, including this jutting slab known as the Balconies. The region was long the home of Aborigines and the park contains many Aboriginal art sites that feature 4000 paintings. Most of these are in red ochre and depict animals, stick-like figures and hand stencils. The local Koori history and culture is explained at the Brambuk Living Cultural Centre near the area's main settlement of Halls Gap.

Right The flora and fauna of the Grampians region are renowned. The spring wildflowers are of particular note, with blooms such as the pink heath (Victoria's floral emblem), orchids, and a unique Grampian shrub creating a riot of colour from June to November. There are koalas and kangaroos here, and also the rare smoky mouse.

Port Campbell National Park

Following pages Port Campbell is a peaceful cove, safe for swimming and boating, tucked quietly in amongst a treacherous coastline. The Port Campbell National Park runs along the wild coastline of Victoria's south-west, a strip of land that is lashed by the wild Southern Ocean. It is one of the continent's most dramatic seascapes. There is nothing to separate the fierce sea and winds from chilly Antarctica, and the relentless weathering of the fragile limestone rock has created some amazingly sheer cliffs and offshore rocks. With titles like Island Arch, Loch Ard Gorge, the Twelve Apostles and London Bridge, the names sound almost as spectacular as the formations themselves appear.

Tasman Peninsula

Above On the island of Tasmania's east coast, Freycinet National Park is a remarkable wonderland of sheer cliffs and headlands, surf, and delightful white sandy beaches. The reddish granite rocks of this peninsula have been battered by winds and waves into deeply indented forms, while dense coastal scrub and heathland dominate areas away from the coast. To the south of the peninsula, and separated by a kilometre of sea, Schouten Island rises dramatically from the ocean. Although extremely rocky in parts, this uninhabited island, which was added to the national park in 1967, also features tranquil bays and beaches.

Right Perfectly shaped Wineglass Bay must be the most photographed area of the 13 000ha (32 123 acres) Freycinet National Park. The quartzite sand is incredibly white, the waters are azure, and the bay is surrounded by hills and vegetation. Other coves and beaches like curved Honeymoon Bay are almost as spectacular, and the park is also home to eucalypt forest, wonderful wildflowers in spring, prolific birdlife, and fauna such as wombats, wallabies and brush-tailed possums.

Below South of Freycinet National Park and east of Hobart, the coastline bulges and curves as it takes on the shape of two peninsulas – the Forestier and the Tasman – which are linked by a narrow strip of land known as Eaglehawk Neck. This wave-pounded area is famous for its unusual and heavily eroded rock formations, such as the Devil's Kitchen, Tasman Arch and the Blowhole, and its tessellated pavement. This rock platform, composed of mudstone, has been weathered by the sea into neat, patterned blocks which look more like the work of man than nature.

Tasmania's historic sites

Left On the southern edge of the Tasman Peninsula, Port Arthur is one of Australia's most tragic but fascinating historic sites. This was the setting for a large penal settlement that was established in 1830, and the scene of hard labour and a harsh life for more than 12 000 male convicts sent from Britain, Sydney and other parts of the colony in the period up to 1877. The men worked in chain gangs, lived in a prison and often received large numbers of lashes for misdemeanours. Featuring 30 or so historic buildings and sites, including this impressive church, a 'model' prison, and the settlement's eerie burial ground, the Isle of the Dead, Port Arthur is a leading tourist attraction as well as a reminder of Australia's often brutal early days.

Above Cascade Brewery (1824) is home to popular Cascade beer. This view of the brewery, Australia's oldest, also shows the lower slopes of Mount Wellington, Hobart's imposing and windswept 1270m-high (4167ft) peak which dominates the city. Founded 16 years after Sydney in 1804, Tasmania's major settlement of Hobart is the nation's second-oldest capital city. With its cool climate, slow pace of life and charming streets and buildings, Hobart is more European in style than most Australian cities. Home even today to less than 200 000 people, this history-packed capital has retained many fine old buildings, like the Cascade Brewery, many early 1830s homes, churches and warehouses, and the atmospheric 1837 Theatre Royal.

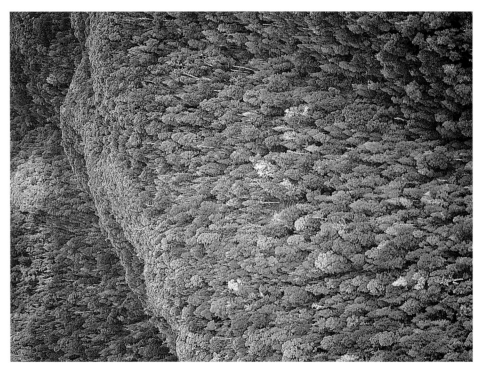

Tasmania's World Heritage parks

Above A large section of Tasmania – almost 1.4 million hectares (3.5 million acres) – falls under UNESCO World Heritage protection in recognition of the beauty and ecological significance of the unique wilderness areas of the island's west and south. In addition to the Cradle Mountain–Lake St Clair region to the north and the remote Southwest National Park in the south, a large part of this protected area is taken up by the Franklin–Gordon Wild Rivers National Park. This reserve is a pristine and unpopulated environment of raging rivers, peaks, rainforest and high moorland. One of the park's highlights is 1443m-high (4734ft) Frenchmans Cap (above), a sheer quartzite peak that towers over the Franklin River valley, where the adventurous can tackle one of the world's best white-water-rafting experiences.

Above right West of the Franklin–Gordon Wild Rivers National Park, the high west coast rainfall belt has given rise to some of the world's most dense and beautiful temperate rainforest. The hills, ridges and valleys of this area, surrounding the port and fishing town of Strahan, receive around 2000mm (79in) of rain each year and are blanketed with Huon pines and other slow-growing coniferous trees that can be as much as 2000 years old. Settlers, attracted by the vast amounts of timber, moved into this region in the 1820s and the forests were logged extensively. Thankfully, with much of this area under national park and World Heritage care, large sections of these unique forests have been saved from obliteration. This west coast region has also been mined extensively, with gold, silver, copper, lead, and zinc extracted from the ground for many decades.

Right Another delightful facet of the Tasmanian west coast region around Strahan is the unspoilt coastline. This is where the frequently wild Southern Ocean, stirred by the prevailing winds, lashes the headlands and beaches. Located on the inlet of Macquarie Harbour, the tiny port and holiday town of Strahan is also the main access point for cruises on the famous brown waters of the Gordon River – a colouring that is caused by staining from the surrounding forests and peat bogs. With an area of about 285km² (110 sq miles) Macquarie Harbour is a vast sheltered waterway, surrounded by thickly forested hills, which was first visited by Europeans in 1815. The harbour later became the site of a notoriously brutal penal settlement at Sarah Island, where convicts laboured under appalling conditions from 1821 until 1833.

Following pages In Tasmania's central north and also part of the island's World Heritage-listed area, the Walls of Jerusalem National Park forms a superb, stark upland wilderness. This mountain area, an upland plain and range of peaks to the west of the island's Central Plateau, is characterised by sheer, craggy dolerite cliffs, small lakes and particularly hardy vegetation – including heathland plants and snow gums that have been bent and twisted by the strong winds. The 'Walls' themselves form a dramatic, towering amphitheatre of weathered rock which has become an increasingly popular destination for experienced bushwalkers. The national park also contains one of Tasmania's last remaining stands of pencil pines. These trees can be as much as 1000 years old and are strictly protected, as far as possible, from logging, fire or any other damage.

Cradle Mountain–Lake St Clair National Park

Above and below Listed as part of Tasmania's World Heritage region in 1982, the Cradle Mountain–Lake St Clair National Park contains some spectacular alpine scenery. It features peaks, high rocky outcrops, valleys, lakes and tarns, high moorland and unique vegetation. Mount Ossa, the state's highest mountain at 1617m (5305ft), is within the national park, as is 1545m-high (5069ft) Cradle Mountain. Lake St Clair, Australia's deepest lake, reaches a depth of 200m (656ft).

The Overland Track, Tasmania's most famous long-distance walking trail, winds for 80km (50 miles) through the national park. The walk takes 5–10 days and is not for the faint-hearted – unpredictable weather including rain, cold temperatures and even summer sleet or snow are a common feature of the state's highlands. Visitors can enjoy the park with less hardship, however, by staying at the famous Cradle Mountain Lodge, which offers far more comfortable 'eco' experiences.

Above Looking more like a scene from the mountains of Europe, the outlines of Mount Geryon loom above a lake in the Cradle Mountain–Lake St Clair National Park. Although the high peaks are rugged and support very little vegetation, the valleys and more protected areas of the park contain alpine grasses, buttongrass sedgelands and dense forests of trees such as the Tasmanian myrtle and the pencil pine. The valleys' spring and summer wildflowers are quite spectacular, and provide welcome splashes of colour in this often stark environment.

Below Throughout the Cradle Mountain–Lake St Clair National Park, views like this of craggy peaks rising up behind valleys, moorland and stands of Tasmanian trees are a common sight. Wildlife includes native cats, Tasmanian devils, wallabies and wallaby-like pademelons, while the streams are home to the rarely sighted platypus and native trout. Fishing is permitted in season, as long as visitors hold a permit. Bushwalking, hiking and rock climbing are popular, and in winter the rugged terrain is perfect for adventurous cross-country skiing.

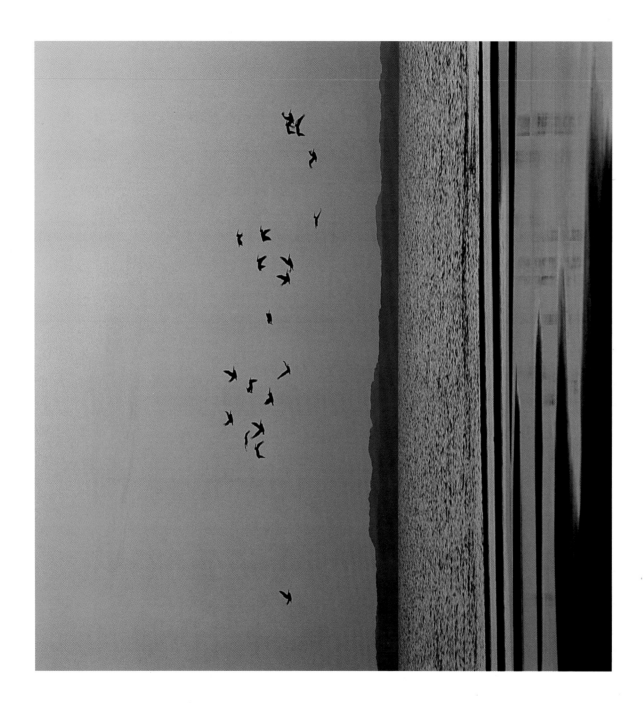

Coorong National Park

Above The Coorong, a long, thin and very saline lagoon, extends for 145km (90 miles) along the South Australian coast, squeezed between the mainland and the equally long stretch of sand and dunes known as the Younghusband Peninsula. This region, encompassed by the Coorong National Park, is known for its prolific birdlife – over 400 species frequent the area, particularly coastal birds that are attracted to this water-dominated environment in their thousands. Australian pelicans are common here, as are seagulls, cormorants, ibises, grebes, spoonbills and black swans. The Coorong pelicans make up Australia's largest such permanent colony, and as many as 5000 of these birds breed here at any one time. Many of the lagoon's islands are breeding grounds for these birds and others, and visitors are requested to keep their distance from such areas. At sunset, a flock of pelicans (above) makes its way back to its nesting ground.

Right South Australia is the nation's driest state but, ironically, its south-eastern coastline is riddled with lakes and waterways. This is where the continent's longest river, the Murray, finally enters the sea after its 2500km (1554 miles) journey from the highlands of southern New South Wales. The Coorong National Park stretches from the mouth of the Murray to near the town of Kingston, on the way to the Victorian border. Although the Coorong and the region's other lakes form tranquil waterways like these (right), the ocean side of the Younghusband Peninsula is pounded by Southern Ocean storms and waves. The dunes support little more than spinifex and other grasses, but around the marshy lagoon, flora such as paperbarks and grasstrees thrive. This entire area is popular with those who enjoy fishing, boating and birdwatching, and there are a number of Aboriginal remnants, such as large shell middens, within the park.

Flinders Chase National Park, Kangaroo Island

Left and above Off the South Australian coast, 145km-long (90 miles) Kangaroo Island forms a notable wildlife and flora sanctuary with an incredible variety of native fauna. The island is famous for its rugged scenery, which includes windswept heathland, beaches, coves and craggy cliffs. Located in Flinders Chase National Park at the island's western end, the Remarkable Rocks are a group of huge granite boulders that have been sculpted by wind and rain into curiously smooth shapes.

Below Named by explorer Matthew Flinders in 1802 for its great abundance of kangaroos, Kangaroo Island is home to a unique sub-species of its namesake. The western grey kangaroo, which populates most of southern Australia, exhibits a slightly different form here and occurs in Flinders Chase National Park and other parts of the island.

Barossa Valley

Above, centre and below The Barossa Valley, north-east of Adelaide, is regarded as Australia's premier wine-producing region and around 60 per cent of the nation's best wine is produced from the valley's 45 or so wineries. The Barossa was founded in the late 1830s by Lutheran migrants from Germany, and the wine-making skills they developed have led to the establishment of world-famous wineries such as Penfolds, Wolf Blass, Henschke and Hardys.

Right Although viticulture and wine-making predominate (ports and sherries are produced here in addition to red and white wines), the Barossa Valley is not entirely focused on these activities. Wheat, stone fruits and other crops are also grown here, with dried apricots being a local specialty. Surrounded by rolling hills and full of picturesque towns, rural museums and National Trust-listed buildings, the Barossa Valley presents a more gentle face of the often harsh Australian countryside.

The WEST

A LAND APART: THE ANCIENT AND THE NEW

Western Australia, the country's largest state, takes up almost one-third of the continent, and although much of this land can be classified as 'outback', or tropical, the remainder of the state is still vast. The West has spectacular coastlines, mineral-rich uplands, semi-desert, the more gentle contours of the forested and farmed south, and a considerable variation in climate which ranges from the damp, temperate Southern Ocean coast to the intense heat of the far north.

The West is a land apart in numerous ways. There are distinct physical differences from the rest of the country: many of the trees, flowers and animals, such as the marsupial quokka and termite-eating numbat, are unique to the area, and the northern Pilbara region contains the continent's oldest and least changed landforms. The people of the West regard themselves as somewhat removed from other Australians, and the coast was once seen as a separate entity. Long before Europeans were aware of the existence of most of the interior, these 17th- and 18th-century seafarers knew the western coastline well and referred to the land as 'New Holland'. The map is dotted with reminders of the early maritime explorers; for example, the Houtman Abrolhos Islands were named in 1619 by Dutch sailors.

Settlement of the West came about in 1826 when south-coast Albany was founded by a party sent from New South Wales. Perth, then known as the Swan River Colony (named after the black swans that still frequent the river), was established three years later. Unlike many of the eastern cities, Perth was first occupied by free settlers, although the very difficult task of colonising this remote part of the continent later required convict assistance. By the 1840s it appeared that sandy soils, floods, droughts and very little interest on the part of settlers would bring about the colony's demise, but fortunes changed slowly and the existence of the state was saved by agriculture, as well as the later discovery of enormous gold reserves.

Despite this disastrous beginning, the relatively peaceful city of Perth – on the banks of the Swan River, close to wonderful Indian Ocean beaches and with a particularly warm and sunny climate – is regarded as one of Australia's finest urban addresses, as is the nearby historic and atmospheric port of Fremantle. This urban area contains over a million people, a very large proportion of the state's total population of about 1.5 million.

The West's long coast – from the South Australian border to Eighty Mile Beach near Broome – is truly spectacular. At the western end of the Great Australian Bight lie the 1860s town of Esperance, the granite outcrops of Cape Le Grand and Cape Arid national parks, and the fauna haven of the Archipelago of the Recherche. Further towards the west is Albany, once an important whaling station and an ideal location for

Left Ningaloo Reef is one of Western Australia's most magnificent natural features. Protected within the Ningaloo Marine Park, it is the world's largest fringing reef – following the coastline for around 260km (162 miles) and coming as close as 100m (109yd) to the shore. Beneath the Indian Ocean, 220 varieties of colourful coral and 500 fish species thrive around the reef and in the clear waters of its lagoon.

Previous pages The Pinnacles in the Nambung National Park were mistaken by 17th-century Dutch seafarers for the ruins of an ancient city. These golden limestone needles and pillars are, however, the result of erosion caused by wind and the effects of wind-blown sand. Probably formed underground as much as 15 000 years ago, the Pinnacles have become exposed by time and the area's shifting sands.

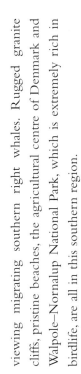

Western Australia's sole World Heritage-listed site is Shark Bay, a large inlet which is famous for the bottlenose dolphins that mingle happily with humans at Monkey Mia. The bay is also rich in other forms of wildlife, including dugongs (the world's only herbivorous marine mammal), turtles, sharks and approximately 310 fish species. This is also the home of the primitive rock-like plants, stromatolites. Australia's first known landfall, when Dutch sailors ventured inland in 1616, took place on the bay's Dirk Hartog Island.

There are more extraordinary coastal features to the north, such as the blowholes and salty Lake MacLeod in the Carnarvon region, the superb beaches of Coral Bay, and Ningaloo Marine Park. Ningaloo encompasses the world's largest fringing coral reef (260km, or 162 miles, long and as close as 100m, or 109yd, to the land in some places) and is a fantastic marine environment of 220 varieties of coral and about 500 different species of fish. Dolphins, dugongs, turtles, migrating humpback whales and whale sharks, the world's biggest fish at up to 18m (59ft) long, also occur here.

Moving further north, the coast takes in the sparsely vegetated limestone terrain of Cape Range National Park, as well as the Burrup Peninsula with its 10 000 or so prehistoric rock engravings, several shell middens and other evidence of Aboriginal occupation. Popular holiday resorts and ports such as Exmouth, Onslow, Dampier, Karratha and the very important Pilbara iron-ore exporting centre of Port Hedland dot this northern coast.

viewing migrating southern right whales. Rugged granite cliffs, pristine beaches, the agricultural centre of Denmark and Walpole–Nornalup National Park, which is extremely rich in birdlife, are all in this southern region.

From Augusta to Perth, the western coast includes the Leeuwin–Naturaliste National Park and its limestone caves, the wine centre of Margaret River, and Geographe Bay with its resorts of Bunbury and Busselton. Just 19km (12 miles) offshore from Fremantle, Rottnest Island is the home of quokkas: small marsupials of the wallaby family unique to Western Australia. Mistaken for rats by 17th-century Dutch seafarers, they are the reason for the island's strange name.

The famous Nambung National Park's 'Pinnacles' occur 250km (155 miles) north of Perth, near the town of Cervantes. These ancient limestone pillars and needles, up to 5m (16ft) high and scattered throughout the desert, have been eroded to form strange, craggy shapes. Nambung also features abundant wildlife including emus, kangaroos and many bird species.

Lying off the central coast are the Houtman Abrolhos Islands, important for lobster fishing, but also a breeding ground for shearwaters, terns and other seabirds. Further north, Kalbarri National Park is a spectacular environment of over 500 plant species. Its surf-pounded coastline, sandstone plains and gorges have been carved out over millions of years by the Murchison River. To the north of Kalbarri lie the wild Zuytdorp Cliffs, part of what Dutch mariners used to call the Batavia coast, which has claimed many ships.

Opposite top left An aerial view of the Hamersley Range in the Pilbara region reveals how rugged and spectacular this ancient upland terrain is: the rocks here are estimated to be 3000 million years old.

Opposite top right The North West Coastal Highway, which follows the coastline from Geraldton to Port Hedland, passes through desolate terrain where strong winds often whip the sand into fierce sandstorms.

Opposite bottom left The incredibly flat Nullarbor Plain stretches across the south of Western Australia into South Australia. This low plateau drops dramatically into the Great Australian Bight in the form of towering limestone cliffs that extend for hundreds of kilometres.

Opposite bottom right Verdant tropical vegetation, such as introduced date palms, and these Livistona (or cabbage tree) palms and water lilies, is a delightful and unexpected feature of the Millstream–Chichester National Park to the north of the arid Pilbara region. Although much of this park is made up of dry rocky ranges and clay tablelands, permanent freshwater springs have given rise to this contrasting environment of lush greenery.

Above Inland from the port of Albany on the south coast, the Stirling Range is one of the state's most impressive mountain chains. These dramatic peaks reach their summit here, at the craggy rocks of the 1073m-high (3521ft) Bluff Knoll.

Although the British had an albeit tenuous foothold in the West by the late 1820s, and the settlers had opened up the agricultural areas around Perth by the 1850s, the remainder of this western region was virtually untouched until 1841. This was the year of Edward John Eyre's pioneering trek from South Australia across the Nullarbor Plain to Albany in search of a route for droving cattle west. Today, the flat, arid and featureless Nullarbor (Latin for 'no trees') is just as inhospitable as it was in Eyre's day. This vast limestone plain, the bed of a 20 million-year-old sea, is riddled with caves, potholes and underground rivers created by rain percolating through the porous rock. Little grows in this waterless desert other than drought-resistant plants such as bluebush and saltbush.

The Nullarbor, which drops abruptly into the Southern Ocean in the form of sheer cliffs, was for a long time a formidable barrier between east and west. The plain was 'conquered', however, by the construction of an overland telegraph line to Perth in the 1870s. Other engineering feats followed in the shape of the 1917 Trans Australian Railway, famous for the world's longest stretch of straight track (478km; 297 miles), and the 1940s Eyre Highway, named after the intrepid explorer.

The famous Western Australian goldfields, where the precious metal was first discovered in the late 1880s, lie to the west of the desolate Nullarbor. This discovery boosted the

West's population and provided a valid reason to venture into the rugged inland. Gold is still mined in reasonably large quantities at Kalgoorlie-Boulder, the region's largest outback town with a population of approximately 23 000. The development of this semi-desert area was extremely difficult, but in 1903 an ingenious 600km-long (373 miles) water pipeline was built, linking the goldfields with Mundaring Weir near Perth. Water still reaches the south of Western Australia via this pipeline.

Although much of the West's inland is arid and flat, the region contains some spectacular hills and mountains. The craggy 65km-long (40 miles) Stirling Range rises to over 1000m (3281ft) inland from Albany, while Perth is backed by the rolling hills of the forested Darling Range. Further north lie the fossil- and gemstone-rich Kennedy Range near Carnarvon and the magnificent 1106m-high (3629ft) Mount Augustus, two and a half times the size of Uluru and the world's largest monolith. The national park here also contains remarkable Aboriginal rock paintings and engravings.

The West's most important upland region, however, is the geologically complex Pilbara and its spectacular Hamersley Range. This 510 000km^2 (196 860 sq miles) desert landscape, with its 3000 million-year-old rocks, encompasses the gorges, mountains, plateaus and rivers of Karijini (Hamersley Range) National Park. One of the state's largest reserves, Karijini is

Above The town of Fremantle, just 20km (12 miles) from Perth, has long been the capital city's major port and fishing centre. Founded in the same year as Perth, it contains many historic buildings.

Below Perth, the Western Australian capital, is a clean city with beautiful beaches, a benign climate and an attractive setting on the Swan River. First settled in 1829, it is home to less than a million people.

rich in Aboriginal sites and hosts a variety of wildlife including echidnas, snakes and many lizard species. Also in the Pilbara, the 200 000ha (494 200 acres) Millstream–Chichester National Park contains basalt ranges, freshwater springs, an oasis of date palms, a large fruit bat colony and important Aboriginal sites.

This whole northern area borders the central deserts and is extremely arid – the Tropic of Capricorn passes a little to the south, and the hamlet of Marble Bar (Australia's hottest place) holds the record of 161 consecutive days of temperatures over 37.8°C (100°F). As with the barren southern goldfields, however, the lure of precious minerals has brought people to

the region. The Pilbara is particularly rich in minerals, with iron ore extracted at Newman and Tom Price, and gold at Mount Magnet and Meekatharra. The latter is also a sheep and cattle-farming centre and an important base for the Royal Flying Doctor Service and School of the Air. Asbestos was mined at Wittenoom (near Newman and Tom Price) until 1966 and travellers are warned to avoid this contaminated area.

The land to the north and east of Perth is far more welcoming and it was in this area that agriculture and related townships were first established – the Avon Valley towns of Northam and York, for example, date from the 1830s. This is also part of the West's vast wheat belt, which stretches east towards the goldfields and south towards the coast, and is the

home of the extraordinary formation known as Wave Rock. This seemingly petrified giant wave – more than 100m (109yd) long and 15m (49ft) high – is, in fact, an overhanging granite wall formed by millions of years of erosion.

Another important agricultural region, specialising in viticulture and timber, is found to the south of Perth. The Margaret River area is famous for its fine wines, and the south-west's unique timber is world renowned. The hard-wood eucalypts such as karri and jarrah that grow around Manjimup, Pemberton and many of the other southern towns are used for shipbuilding and flooring as well as for

high-quality furniture. Thankfully, these unique tall-growing trees are also protected in several reserves and national parks.

The West's uniqueness and separateness is perhaps best illustrated by its incredible range of flora, much of which grows nowhere else in the Australian continent. The state is home to at least 8000 flowering plant species, varying from tiny ground orchids to bizarrely shaped grasstrees and the giant hardwoods. Wildflowers, including the unique red and green kangaroo-paws, blue leschenaultias and various species of dryandras, banksias and carnivorous plants like the drosera (sundew) bloom magnificently from August to November to enhance the West's status as one of the continent's most special and beautiful natural environments.

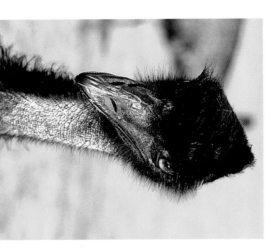

Above left Australia's largest bird, the flightless emu, can reach a height of almost 2m (6.5ft). It inhabits most parts of the Australian continent.

Above centre Found only on Rottnest Island and the far south-west of Western Australia, the quokka is a small marsupial and a member of the wallaby family.

Above right Although very young, this kangaroo exhibits the features that make the species such powerful 'hoppers' – long feet and disproportionately powerful hind legs.

Left Apart from the platypus, the spine-covered echidna is Australia's only surviving example of a monotreme – a primitive form of mammal that lays eggs.

Nullarbor Plain

Above Around 20 million years ago, the flat plain known as the Nullarbor formed the bed of a large sea. Pushed up by geological forces, however, this vast area of 200 000km² (77 200 sq miles) is now a dry and inhospitable plateau. It is the world's largest single piece of limestone, covering a large part of south-east Western Australia and extending well into South Australia. On the surface there is little to break the Nullarbor Plain's monotony – rainfall is minimal and the limestone supports only hardy vegetation – but the subterranean world is different. Sparse rain has soaked through the porous rock over the

millenia and a huge network of potholes, caves and catacombs has been formed. There are even underground rivers here, and the plain is a popular destination for Australia's speleologists.

Right Although the Nullarbor was first explored by Europeans in the early 1840s and has obviously been crossed countless times since, this plain forms an awesome barrier between Western Australia and what its residents often call the 'eastern states' – anything beyond the border! In the last century, particularly, it is easy to understand how this large and arid expanse reinforced the sense of isolation felt by the inhabitants of the west. The Trans Australian Railway to the mining centre of Kalgoorlie was built across the Nullarbor Plain in 1917, and by the 1940s the Eyre Highway had been constructed. However today's travellers still see little more from their windows than a flat expanse broken only by low, drought-resistant scrub and the occasional sand hill.

Wave Rock

Above Aptly named Wave Rock, and near the small agricultural town of Hyden, this is one of the western region's most curious and famous geological formations. At over 100m (109yd) long and 15m (49ft) high this is not in fact a 'rock' at all, but a once-vertical granite wall that has slowly been eroded into a smooth curving shape over as much as 3000 million years. Another factor which adds to Wave Rock's appearance of a cresting wave-like motion is the fact that the concave wall is streaked in colourful vertical bands of earth tones such as rust, red, gold and grey that have been created by rainwater reacting with chemicals within the granite.

Above right Located within a 160ha (395 acres) reserve, Wave Rock understandably attracts visitors in their thousands. The structure above the rock, an unfortunate intrusion on nature's work, is the wall of a water catchment area. The region around Hyden, part of the state's vast wheat belt, contains many other strange formations with equally evocative names such as the Hippo's Yawn and the self-explanatory Breakers and the Humps. Known geologically as inselbergs, these weathered structures are isolated outcrops of the area's vast granite underlay. The Hyden district is also important for its Aboriginal hand stencils on the walls of nearby Mulkas Cave.

Geographe Bay and Leeuwin–Naturaliste National Park

Above The large curve of Geographe Bay, to the south of Perth, was named by French explorers and scientists after one of their ships, the Geographe, which anchored here in 1801. The area's main town of Busselton was first settled 30 years after the visit of the French and grew up as a port for the surrounding agricultural and timber farming area. By the end of the 19th century, Busselton had become a popular seaside resort, and the town is still a favourite holiday destination for Western Australians, as is the nearby town of Dunsborough. Drawcards include the temperate climate, the bay's generally calm waters and attractive beaches, and boating and fishing opportunities. Busselton is also famous for its 2km-long (1.25 miles) jetty, one of Australia's longest. The town is named after the Bussell family, local settlers who have a special claim to fame – Grace Bussell became a national heroine after playing a prominent role in a highly successful rescue effort of a wrecked Geographe Bay ship and its passengers in 1876.

Right South of Cape Naturaliste, which marks the south-western end of Geographe Bay, the Indian Ocean coast stretches south for over 90km (56 miles) to another prominent headland, Cape Leeuwin. Much of this shore and its hinterland, which forms the continent's extreme south-west, is contained within the Leeuwin–Naturaliste National Park – an area of wave-battered cliffs and headlands, beautiful empty beaches and limestone heathland. The windswept clifftops are home to low-growing heath flora, mallee (a hardy form of eucalyptus tree), and scrub, as well as many varieties of seabirds, possums and the western quoll, or native cat. The limestone rock here is riddled with caves and their fantastic formations, and many of these are open to visitors. Further inland there is a large and isolated forest of karri, one of the world's tallest trees, that grows only in south-western Australia and is normally found considerably further east.

Wheat belts and wildflowers

Above The famous wheat belt, covering a vast area of the state's south and west, is Western Australia's agricultural heartland and produces the majority of the state's cereal crops. Throughout this mostly very flat farming region, wheat fields such as these stretch like a lovely golden carpet towards the horizon.

Opposite top North and west of these fertile agricultural lands the area known as the Murchison Goldfields region, around small towns like Mount Magnet, Yalgoo and Paynes Find, becomes much more arid. After rain, however, the apparently barren ground comes alive with ephemerals like 'everlasting' wildflowers, such as these at Mongers Lake.

Opposite centre and bottom Once the wildflowers have died off, the vegetation of Mongers Lake resorts to its normal state – hardy and parched-looking resident plants that are able to survive in the red earth and dry conditions. This region, around the Great Northern Highway, contains dozens of dry lakes, both small and large, as well as many long-abandoned gold-mining townships and diggings. Paynes Find and Yalgoo, for example, were thriving townships in the 1890s and early 1900s, when shops and hotels boomed and the population greatly outnumbered the handful of residents that live there today. This arid area also contains some significant Aboriginal relics, including cave paintings and curious stone formations.

The Pinnacles

Located in Nambung National Park near the small town of Cervantes, 245km (152 miles) north of Perth, the limestone structures called the Pinnacles cover a large area of windblown desert just inland from the ocean. The park contains thousands of these distinctively jagged formations, varying in height and bulk, some of which are 6m (20ft) tall. Visitors can drive around the site on a one-way loop road. Alternatively a short walking track provides the opportunity to get a much closer look at the eroded limestone. Nambung's other attractions are its sandy beaches, excellent fishing, and the chance to observe kangaroos, wallabies, goannas, and some of the area's 90 bird species.

Kalbari National Park

Above and right Located between the town of Geraldton and Shark Bay, Kalbari National Park is one of the west's many natural highlights. It is dominated by its sandstone rock formations and the lower reaches of the Murchison River. On the coast, the cliffs, like these in the area around Island Rock, are capped by a layer of limestone. Erosion has created numerous gorges, such as at Pot Alley (right), and rock formations like Natural Bridge, Red Bluff and Grandstand Rocks.

The coastline has claimed many ships, including the Batavia, which ran aground on the Houtman Abrolhos Islands in 1629. The ensuing mutiny resulted in two of the crew being abandoned in the Kalbari area, making them the continent's first known European residents.

Left In both the coastal and inland regions of Kalbari National Park, the friable sandstone rock has been weathered into interesting shapes, formations and bands of colour. The cream, brown and vivid red sandstone in this area bears the most unusual name of 'tumblagooda'. The park, proclaimed in 1963, features western grey and red kangaroos, rock wallabies, emus and over 170 other species of birds.

Left and top Kalbarri National Park's winding valleys and deep gorges have been carved out by the mighty Murchison River over an incredibly long period of time. Until around 2 million years ago the river flowed over a flat sandstone plain, but subsequent geological movement pushed the earth's crust upwards and the Murchison was then forced to cut deeply into the rock in order to resume its original course. The region now features around 80km (50 miles) of gorges, which visitors can view from the air, or from one of the national park's many lookout points. This view of the gorge, valley and river (top) is from the rock formation called Nature's Window, one of the park's most famous scenic attractions, while a broader panorama (left) takes in the area known as Loop Bend. The 800km-long (497 miles) Murchison River rises far inland, north of the mining and cattle town of Meekatharra, and eventually reaches the sea at Gantheaume Bay — close to the coast's eroded limestone cliffs.

Above This outlook on the river and the flat sand plains is from the Hawks Head lookout; visitors often attempt to pick out the well-known rock formation, in the shape of a hawk, from this point. The Murchison River may look extremely placid here, but after the heavy summer rains it is transformed into a raging torrent, demonstrating its awesome erosive powers as it passes through the canyons that are up to 70m (230ft) deep. The sandy plains support many shrubs and small trees, and an extraordinary variety of wildflowers; the national park contains more than 500 plant species.

The Zuytdorp Cliffs

North of Kalbarri National Park, the rugged and isolated coastline continues in the form of the famed Zuytdorp Cliffs, part of what Dutch explorers and seafarers christened the 'Batavia Coast'. This wild stretch, notorious for its reputation as a graveyard for ships, was named after either the province of Batavia (now Jakarta), or the ship of the same name which ran aground on the reefs of the nearby Houtman Abrolhos Islands in the early 1600s. The cliffs take their name from the

wreck of another Dutch ship, the Zuytdorp, which met its end here in 1712 en route to the East Indies. This ship, discovered only in the 1950s, still lies offshore but some of her historic artefacts are on display in the Maritime Museum at Geraldton, further south.

Viewed from the air, the cliffs reveal blowholes at their base (above), and a long line of sheer rock fringed by blue waters and foaming surf. Inland, the plain leads east towards the North West Coastal Highway.

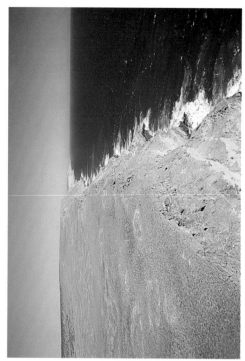

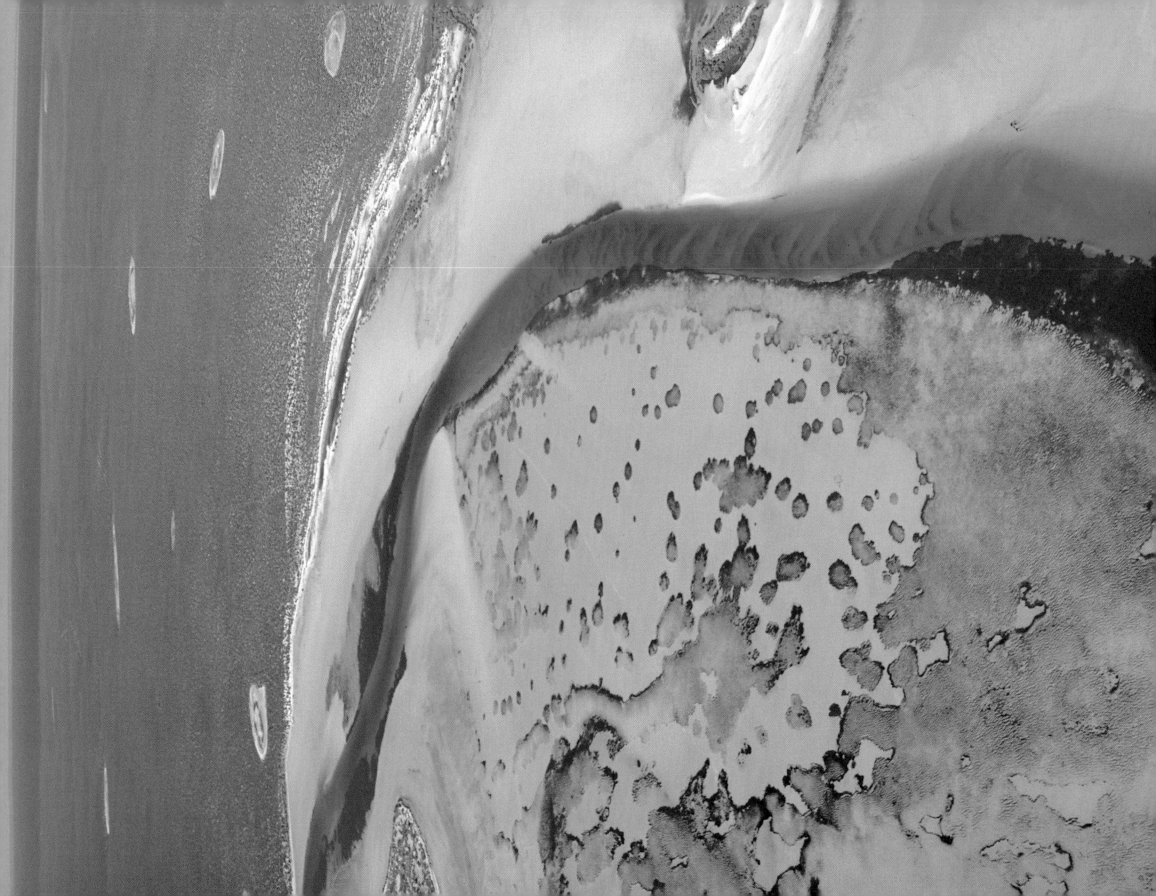

Shark Bay

Left Shark Bay a huge salty inlet dotted with islands, peninsulas and lagoons 700km (435 miles) north of Perth, forms one of the world's most extraordinary marine wonderlands – the region is of such significance that it has been World Heritage-listed, and also preserved within the Shark Bay Marine Park. The bay's highlights include the ancient stromatolites – some of the world's oldest life forms – that grow in the Hamelin Pool Marine Nature Reserve, and 110km-long (68 miles) Shell Beach. This is one of just two beaches worldwide that is composed of non-fossilised shells; reaching a depth of up to 10m (33ft), these shells have been formed by countless numbers of tiny white molluscs.

Dirk Hartog Island is of great historic significance. This was the site of Australia's first known landfall by Europeans. On 25 October 1616 Dutch mariners from the Eendracht landed here and recorded the event on a metal plaque at Cape Inscription. A replica is now displayed in the Western Australian Maritime Museum in Fremantle.

Above and below Shark Bay encompasses 1500km (932 miles) of coastline that includes the Peron Peninsula, named after a naturalist on the French ship Geographe which visited the area south of Perth in the early 1800s. On the peninsula, the bay's main settlement of Denham is Australia's most westerly town and also a centre for the tourists who come to witness one of Australia's most intriguing natural wonders. Nearby, at Monkey Mia, very sociable bottlenose dolphins regularly come to the shore to meet, be touched by, and frolic with visitors. Other inhabitants of Shark Bay include dugongs, whales, manta rays and turtles, and around 300 fish species. One of the reasons for this proliferation of marine life is the presence of vast beds of seagrass that cover large areas of the bay. The Peron Peninsula also includes the Francois Peron National Park, once an incredibly remote sheep station, but now home to seagulls and a wide variety of other birdlife, and featuring numerous salt lakes that contain gypsum deposits.

The Carnarvon coastline

Seventy kilometres (43 miles) north of the fishing town of Carnarvon, the coast surrounding remote Quobba Station contains extensive blowholes that were discovered only in 1911. The limestone rocks here feature large holes through which the pounding Indian Ocean forces its way with tremendous pressure, creating spectacular water jets of up to 20m (66ft) high. The Carnarvon area is also famous for its enormous king waves and tides that regularly sweep the coastline – the evidence of which can be seen (right) near Quobba Station. Other interesting features of the Carnarvon coastal region include a hot-water bore, several freshwater swimming holes and the vast Lake MacLeod, a generally dry, below-sea-level lake where salt has been mined, aided by the process of evaporation and subsequent crystallisation, since the 1960s. Despite this industrial activity, the lake is also a noted bird sanctuary.

Karijini National Park

Left Formerly called the Hamersley Range National Park but now known by its Aboriginal name of Karijini, this reserve in the Pilbara region contains some of Western Australia's most spectacular scenery. Featuring ancient mountains, high plateaus, rivers and deep gorges, as well as one of the state's highest peaks – 1235m-high (4052ft) Mount Bruce — the park is home to a variety of wildlife. Echidnas, snakes, brush-tailed wallabies, goannas, dingoes and abundant bird species all inhabit the area. The weathered walls of Dales Gorge are one of the park's highlights, and this popular destination for visitors also offers camping facilities and a walking track that takes in pools, waterfalls and tropical vegetation.

Below Karijini National Park's Aboriginal connections run deep. The ranges here are the traditional home of several local clans, there is a large tract of Aboriginal-owned land nearby, and the park's new name was chosen in consultation with the people. A modern trend, as also evidenced at Uluru in the Northern Territory, is to encourage the indigenous people to become involved with the national parks movement, and Karijini employs some Aboriginal rangers. It seems entirely appropriate that the original custodians of this ancient landscape are on hand to explain and protect its history, traditions, flora and fauna.

Above and right Karijini National Park is renowned for its quite spectacular and often very narrow gorges that are as much as 100m (328ft) deep. These include Hancock Gorge (above) and Joffre Gorge (right), where a waterfall tumbles over the deep red cliff after periods of high rainfall. Many of these chasms feature shady waterholes that are popular with visitors seeking respite from the sun. The bright light here often makes the already deep-red rock walls glow with a fiery intensity. *The Pilbara rocks, creating such dramatic scenery in the national park, have another important purpose: minerals, particularly vast amounts of iron ore, are extracted from the ground at mines in and around the nearby towns of Tom Price and Newman, while Wittenoom, just outside the park, was the site of asbestos mining until the 1960s.*

Millstream–Chichester National Park

Previous pages Although close to Karijini National Park and composed of similar Pilbara rocks, Millstream–Chichester National Park presents a very different scene. From here there are extensive views north over the coastal plain and towards the town of Roebourne, and the park contains a much greater variety of vegetation. Rivers, permanent pools and waterholes have given rise to lush greenery. Other highlights include the park's more arid tablelands and basalt ranges, and excellent views of the waterways and surrounding forest from various lookouts. The region is of great importance to the local Aboriginal people, who still visit the area for food-gathering and special rituals.

Left Australia's most common animal is the kangaroo (the continent's marsupials are virtually unique). This mother and her offspring are from the Millstream–Chichester National Park. Like wallabies, koalas, possums and wombats, they are marsupials — non-placental mammals that give birth to tiny, almost embryonic, young which spend most of their developmental stage in the mother's abdominal pouch, or *marsupium*. The pouch contains the female's mammary glands, to which the young become firmly attached. Even when developed, juvenile kangaroos, known as 'joeys', often take refuge in the pouch.

Burrup Peninsula

Top left and right Named after the famous English explorer and seafarer William Dampier, who visited this region in the late 17th century, the town of Dampier and the nearby Dampier Archipelago are two major features of the rugged Pilbara coast. Although the 1960s town of Dampier is primarily a port for the export of iron ore, the 42 islands making up the archipelago form a remarkable nature reserve. North-east of Dampier lies the Burrup Peninsula, a region composed of red rocks and sandy beaches that was an island until linked to the mainland by a causeway. Now used primarily by a natural-gas-drilling operation, the peninsula is of great Aboriginal historical and cultural significance.

Bottom left and right The Burrup Peninsula contains well over 100 000 Aboriginal rock engravings at some 500 sites, making the area one of the richest of such prehistoric art locations in the Australian continent — and probably the world. In addition to the rather simplified carvings and etchings of emus, kangaroos and several other birds and animals, the Burrup Peninsula also features fish traps and shell middens — often huge piles of discarded shells — that reveal much about the eating habits of the Aboriginal people of the past.

The Pilbara region

Left Snappy gums, such as these growing in Millstream–Chichester National Park, are quite a common feature of this region and are also found throughout the northern parts of the Northern Territory and western Queensland. Like the river red gum, this tree is well adapted to dry conditions and is often found growing, as here, on rocky hills and outcrops. With their smooth white trunks, small greyish-green leaves, straggly growth and low stature, these trees rarely grow above 7m (23ft) in height. Snappy gums are a distinctive feature of the continent's moderate- to low-rainfall areas.

Above At dusk and under the moonlight, a river red gum in the Pilbara region takes on the reddish colours of the surrounding land. These drought-resistant eucalyptus trees are widespread throughout Australia's arid and semiarid regions – growing anywhere from the banks of the Murray River in South Australia and western Victoria to as far north and west as the Pilbara. Characterised by their wide spread of branches and thick trunks, river red gums generally feature smooth bark and, despite their name, are of a predominantly blue-grey or pale yellow colour.

Eighty Mile Beach

Following pages At the northernmost edge of the Australian continent's west, Eighty Mile Beach – which is actually 137km (85 miles) long – is located beyond the harbour of Port Hedland. The incredibly white sands and turquoise waters here are usually deserted as few tourists pass through this very remote area. Inland lies the Great Northern Highway, bordering the coast en route to the tropical town of Broome, while beyond the road is the vast arid expanse of the uninhabited Great Sandy Desert. Minerals and mining are virtually the only reasons why non-Aboriginal people live in this northern region of Western Australia; vast amounts of iron ore, in particular, are extracted from mines at Newman and Tom Price and shipped around the world from Port Hedland.

INDEX

Above The famous stage curtain of Kuranda's Tjapukai Dance Theatre.

PHOTOGRAPHIC CREDITS

Above A kurrajong tree casts a cool shadow on this ancient red rock in the Pilbara region of Western Australia.

Copyright © of the photographs rests with the following photographers and/or their agents:

Shaen Adey (NHAIL): jacket spine, endpapers (top row: left; second row: second from left; third row: left, second from left, right; bottom row: second from left), pp. 1, 4/5, 13 (bottom), 15, 17 (bottom centre), 18 (top), 23, 25 (bottom), 32 (top right, bottom right), 33, 35 (left), 42 (bottom left & right), 42/43 (top), 43 (bottom left), 46, 50, 51, 53, 54, 55, 64, 65, 66, 67, 73 (top), 77, 78, 79, 80, 81 (top), 82, 83, 84, 86/87, 90, 91, 92/93, 94, 95, 100 (bottom), 101 (bottom), 115 (top), 116, 117, 118, 119, 128, 129, 130, 131, 132, 133, 151, 186 (top left, top right, bottom right), 189 (top right), 196, 198, 199 (bottom), 200 (top), 201, 202, 203, 204, 205, 208, 209, 214/215, 216, 217, 222; **Australian Museum (NF):** p. 22 (bottom); **Bill Bachman (PI):** pp. 32 (top left), 44 (left), 207 (top), 220/221, 224; **Ross Barnett:** pp. 3, 70, 74, 85 (right), 102, 142, 143, 144, 150 (top left), 156, 163 (bottom), 179 (bottom); **Colin Beard:** back cover (bottom right), pp. 32 (bottom left), 108/109, 113, 114 (bottom), 124 (centre left & right), 135 (bottom), 138, 139, 162, 164/165; **John Borthwick:** p. 81 (bottom); **Peter D. Canty:** pp. 134, 135 (top & centre), 186 (bottom left), 190, 191; **Evan Collis (PI):**

pp. 187, 192, 193; **Kerry Cook (PI):** p. 207 (bottom); **Kevin Deacon (OEI):** p. 61 (centre & bottom); **Chris Garnett (PI):** back cover (top left), pp. 12, 218, 219; **Michael Gebicki:** pp. 62 (left), 122; **P. German (NF):** p. 189 (bottom); **Catherine H. Gibbons (Frontline):** p. 114 (top); **Leigh Hemmings:** pp. 19, 96, 120; **IOA (Frontline):** pp. 180, 181; **Richard I'Anson:** back cover (bottom left), pp. 14 (bottom), 21, 24 (top), 30, 59, 73 (bottom), 103, 125, 127, 146/147, 157, 160 (bottom), 161, 163 (top), 168; **Michael James (PI):** p. 188 (top); **Anthony Johnson (NHAIL):** endpapers (top row: second from left; second row: right), pp. 2, 26, 35 (right), 58, 101 (top right), 110, 115 (bottom), 152, 153, 169, 170, 171; **Ford Kristo:** p. 72; **Roel Loopers (PI):** p. 39 (top right); **David McGonigal:** endpapers (bottom row: left), pp. 18 (bottom), 41, 43 (bottom right), 47 (right), 97 (right), 148, 174 (top); **Geoff McKell (PI):** front cover; **Leo Meier (APL):** pp. 34, 56, 57, 63; **NHAIL:** p. 27 (bottom); **Nick Rains:** pp. 104, 105, 107, 112 (bottom); **Mark Rajkovic:** p. 166 (bottom); **Col Roberts (PI):** pp. 28/29, 36, 37, 38, 39 (bottom), 45; **Paul Sinclair:** endpapers (top row: right; second row: second from right; bottom row: second from right), pp. 10, 20, 88, 89, 106, 145 (right), 154, 155, 158, 159, 178, 179 (top); **Paul Steel:** endpapers

(third row: second from right), pp. 16 (bottom centre), 68/69, 75, 98/99, 100 (top), 188 (bottom); **Paul Steel (PI):** pp. 182/183, 199 (top); **Ann Storrie (PI):** p. 194 (left); **David Tatnall:** endpapers (top row: second from right), pp. 121, 160 (top); **Liz Thompson:** pp. 24 (bottom), 123, 126; **Michael Trenerry (NF):** p. 16 (top); **Cherie Vasas (NT&MI):** pp. 60, 61 (top); **Gerry Velaitis (Frontline):** endpapers (second row: left; bottom row: right), pp. 13 (top), 136, 137, 172/173, 175 (top), 176, 177; **Peter Vorlicek:** p. 17 (top); **Dave Watts (NF):** pp. 16 (bottom left & right), 17 (bottom left), 150 (bottom); **Babs & Bert Wells (NF):** p. 17 (bottom right); **John Whitfield-King (PI):** p. 189 (top centre); **Dick Whitford (NF):** p. 22 (top); **Wildside:** pp. 6/7, 27 (top), 48/49, 52, 76, 112 (top), 124 (top & bottom), 140/141, 150 (top right), 166 (top), 167, 174 (bottom), 175 (bottom), 189 (top left), 210, 211, 212, 213; **Richard Wölendorp (PI):** back cover (top right), pp. 14 (top), 25 (top), 40, 184, 195, 197, 200 (bottom), 206.

APL = Australian Picture Library; IOA = Images of Adelaide, NF = Nature Focus, NHAIL = New Holland Australia Image Library, NT&MI = Nature Travel and Marine Images, OEI = Ocean Earth Images, PI = Photo Index.